SIRRO!

Tales from Tiger Town

SIRRO!

Tales from Tiger Town

**PAUL SIRONEN
WITH DANIEL LANE**

an
ABC
BOOK

Published by ABC Books for the
AUSTRALIAN BROADCASTING CORPORATION
GPO Box 9994 Sydney NSW 2001

First published 1997

National Library of Australia
Cataloguing-in-Publication entry
    Sironen, Paul.
    Sirro : tales from Tiger town.

    ISBN 0 7333 0577 6.

    1. Sironen. Paul. 2. Rugby League football players - New South
    Wales - Biography. I. Lane, Daniel (Daniel Q.). II. Australian
    Broadcasting Corporation. III. Title.

796.3338092

Edited by Glenda Downing
Designed by Robert Taylor, Three Doors Typographic Design
Photography by Rugby League Week *unless otherwise indicated*
Set in 10/13 pt Caslon by
Midland Typesetters, Maryborough, Victoria
Colour separations by First Media, Adelaide
Printed and bound in Australia by
Australian Print Group, Maryborough, Victoria

5 4 3 2 1

DEDICATION

*I dedicate this book in the loving memory of my sister-in-law,
Brooke. You were taken away from us all too early in life.*

ACKNOWLEDGMENTS

To Lee-Anne, Curtis and Bayley, without you all this would be worthless; to Mum, Dad, Rod and Aila thanks for giving me a great start in life; Carol, Marc and Corey thanks for your constant support and to the following people I also offer a huge vote of thanks: all the guys I've played alongside; my many coaches, trainers, rubbers, strappers and supporters; my work colleagues at Sport M; my former workmates in the police force; my close friends especially Mudguts, Cully and Thommo; Roy and HG (see you at Club Nude in the off-season); all the gang at Lowes; the media brigade who have given me a pat on the back or a kick up the backside whenever it has been warranted; Kay MacPherson, Les Hobbs and Steve Lockhardt for getting me on the paddock; Keith Barnes for teaching me about haggling; Stuart Neal of ABC books for encouraging me to write a book.

Many thanks to *Rugby League Week* for supplying the bulk of the photographs in this book. Unless otherwise indicated photos are from *Rugby League Week*.

ABOUT DANIEL LANE

My 'ghost' Daniel Lane helped me get this all down on paper. Daniel works full-time at *Rugby League Week*'s Sydney office as a senior journalist. Apart from covering the Sirro years Daniel was named Australia's Junior Sportswriter of the Year in 1986 and in 1990 he won the New South Wales Rugby League's news story award for exposing the game's drug problem. Lane has also written three other books—*Rugby League Rebel—The Mark Geyer Story* (1994), *Laurie and Clyde, Young Guns of Rugby League* (1995) and *A Family Betrayal—One Man's Super League War* (1996).

CONTENTS

Foreword   ix

1 Old Man Tiger   1

2 From Shot-putter to Teenage Shocker   6

3 Childhood Dreams   15

4 Down and Out in Waikiki   23

5 Balmain Blue Heeler   30

6 The Rookie   38

7 The Battler   48

8 Grand Final Heartache   51

9 More Tears and Heartache   61

10 Singin' the Blues   70

11 The Kangaroo Kid   76

12 Friends and Critics   86

13 Money Matters   90

14 Roy, HG ... and My Life As Ian   97

15 The Form Guide   106

16 Best of the Best   119

17 The Clipboard Brigade   137

18 Uncle Sirro's Advice Column   150

19 The Super League Struggle   163

20 The Family Man   169

21 Lee-Anne's Say   171

22 Profile   173

23 The Sirro Roast   176

FOREWORD

I can't really remember the first time I saw Paul Sironen play the Rugby League. I can vaguely remember reading about Paul being extremely fast for his size and being introduced to Gridiron. But I can vividly remember when he arrived in Rugby League, because there followed an enduring series of wild moments of brutal power culminating in a Test performance against a hapless French touring party in a Test match in Parkes, New South Wales, where Paul caught the ball from the opening kickoff and smashed his way ninety metres downfield leaving a startled train of sprawling, bruised Frenchmen, psychologically damaged irreparably. Within his thirty seconds of mayhem the Test match was, in effect, over. This kind of performance was to become expected over a period of many winters for Balmain, New South Wales and Australia. And very often it was delivered.

H. G. Nelson nicknamed Paul 'The Buttocks' during a State Of Origin match, not that he had big buttocks in particular, but it was just a word that sort of suited him. It had a semi-abstract quality that touched a nerve. I think he enjoyed the nickname which was against the trend. His playing partner Benny Elias, from all accounts hated being called 'Backdoor Benny', for example. And I think that in all probability, having been nick-named 'The Buttocks' automatically forced people to spend time examining Paul's buttocks looking for that tell tale angle that would reveal a really huge arse. There wasn't such an angle. As well as being extremely fit, schematically herculean and a football-ing champion, the lenses of cameras liked him and he would appear in newspapers in his policeman's uniform and be seen doing community work. Then we worked with him in the mini soap opera 'Ian' and found Ian to be a really likeable, gentle, humorous fellow. Just like Paul. It was tremendous casting. And tremendous fun working with him.

And then the Balmain club for whom Paul had always played was under pressure to merge with another club or die, and there was a lot of pressure on the quality players, like Paul, to take the vast sums of money being offered by the richer ARL clubs, and then by the Super League clubs, but Paul liked being with the blokes and the club colours he'd been with all his playing life and wanted to play out the rest of his career with them, knowing there may well be an Indian summer among the stolen winters ahead.

And that's what he's doing. Sirro has always played football for the rarest and most honourable of reasons.

John Doyle

OLD MAN TIGER

CHAPTER 1

M inutes after Balmain was narrowly beaten 14–10 in our opening match of the 1997 season by Manly—the ARL's defending premiers, of all bloody teams—a young journalist from the local rag shoved a tape recorder under my nose and asked me to reflect on my twelve years with the Tigers. The kid wanted to know what those years meant to me and God knows, that was a tall order because I'd just busted a gut against the tough Sea Eagles pack and not only was I sweating like a pig but I was exhausted—mentally and physically.

My entire day had been an emotional roller-coaster ride since, in the lead up to the game, I genuinely feared I was in grave danger of making a goose of myself. You see, my off-season had been shot to pieces by a family tragedy and compounding that was the after effects of minor knee surgery which prevented me from ripping and tearing into things on the training paddock. It was a far cry from the kind of build-up I'd have preferred, and when I packed my kitbag before the match it felt as though a net full of butterflies were undergoing electric shock treatment in my stomach. To add further to my despair was the significance of the game. Firstly, it marked Balmain's return to Leichhardt Oval after two bleak winters at Parramatta Stadium, and second, the club had made a bit of a song and dance about my becoming a member of the Tigers' 200 match club. While I'm not an overly superstitious player the ballyhoo the club made in the press about my milestone seemed to set the stage for me to put myself on show—and in the worst possible way.

Even the traffic seemed to be against me because my wife Lee-Anne and I were stuck in bumper-to-bumper traffic on the way to Leichhardt. I hadn't been caught in one on a match day for years and while I'd have gone off my head at the inconvenience in my 'younger' days, as an old man Tiger I simply took time out to reflect on what had been a terrible summer, the absolute lowest point of which had been the highly publicised death of Lee-Anne's eighteen-year-old sister, Brooke. She was one of four people run down by a car outside the Birkenhead Tavern at Drummoyne, and the sense-lessness of her death angered me and it destroyed poor Lee-Anne and her family. At the time of my writing this book, in early 1997, the matter is still before the court and so I'm prevented by law from saying too much about the case except that it was reported Brooke died as a result of the massive injuries she received after running onto the road to help her brother, Marc, after he'd been allegedly run down by a drunk and unlicensed motorist. Witnesses said after hitting Marc and his mate, the driver then did a U-turn and ploughed into poor little Brooke and another person as they tried to drag Marc to safety. Brooke, who was only a kid of eighteen—and a gorgeous kid to boot—lapsed into a coma and never woke up. It was terrible, and losing her has rocked all our lives. The priest who conducted Brooke's funeral said her death was the ultimate act of love, and he quoted a passage from the Bible, John 15:13, to explain what he meant. It said: 'Greater love than this, no one has, than they lay down their life for their friend.' And he was right—young Brooke died courageously, but, sweet Jesus Christ, she shouldn't have had to . . .

I'd had other problems that summer and while they paled hopelessly in comparison with Brooke's death, they were still problems. I'd had my knee scraped in late October and that prevented me from doing much training with the boys, because I hobbled about for weeks like an old grandpa rooster with arthritis. And just as I'd braced myself to throw everything into training, Brooke was killed and my only priority was to help Lee-Anne and our family come to terms with the tragedy. During that time I did some training, but it was only minimal stuff. I also didn't participate in any of the Tigers' trial matches because 'Junior' Pearce figured it was better to let the knee fully heal for the 'real' stuff that lay ahead.

And when the 'real' stuff came along, I was informed it would be against the defending premiers Manly. I knew that would be a real ordeal because apart from having endured a half-baked off-season, I also hadn't played since the last July when I broke my bloody thumb! The whole thing had turned into a nightmare of a challenge and I considered the task of matching muscle with the Sea Eagles' upfront men—Mark Carroll, Steve Menzies, David Gillespie, Jim Serdaris, Daniel Gartner and Nik Kosef—in my condition was akin to being handed a slingshot with the orders to hold off the Red Army. So, as I sat in our car in the traffic, I wondered how on earth I was going to survive the night . . .

The funny thing was, as soon as I walked through the old Leichhardt Oval turnstiles those butterflies and doubts quickly disappeared. I found myself confronted by some familiar faces, and most of them were wearing faded Balmain jumpers from ten or more years ago. I heard a few of them shout out 'Onya Sirro', and while it may sound corny, my worries subsided because it felt as though I was home again, and, even more importantly, it felt as if I was among friends, such as the twenty-odd old East Ryde boys who gave me heaps as I walked towards the dressing rooms. I also noticed people who hadn't been to a Balmain game since we ruled the roost during our glory days standing about and discussing the new breed of Tigers—Mark Stimson, Darren Senter, Glenn Morrison, 'Bubba' Kennedy and Greg Donaghy. It was a magic feeling and it certainly helped to stir the competitive spirit deep within me.

After I finished taping my ears in readiness for battle, the club's marketing people informed me that I was to run through a banner the supporters' club had made to help celebrate my 200th game in the black and gold, and my immediate reaction was to pray the same mob who made the one Garry Jack bounced off a few years ago weren't responsible for mine. I could clearly remember how—much to everyone's delight—Jimmy bounced off the reinforced paper and hit the ground.

As I waited for my cue to charge out of the players' tunnel, I felt more like Humphrey B. Bear than a grizzled old Balmain prop. Then I heard the ground announcer tell the mob: *'If you don't cheer loudly enough, Sirro's not going to come out tonight!'*

Well, they did cheer, and running out onto the oval with what felt like 18 000 'mates' giving me their wholehearted support was pretty bloody special. I'm told once you reach a certain stage in your life some things stand out in your memory and I'm sure that moment will be one of mine, because I almost thought I'd stepped back into time when Balmain were *the* Sydney team and my team-mates, such as Wayne Pearce, Steve Roach, Benny Elias, Garry Jack, Kerry Hemsley and David Brooks, ranked among the game's genuine stars. However, that thought was derailed when I suddenly realised I was the only person on the ground! I didn't know what to do after I finished waving so I started to run back towards the tunnel, and that was when my team-mates decided to run out onto the field. Thanks fellas, another gee-up. But the atmosphere was terrific and the last time I could recall a Balmain crowd chanting 'Tii-gerrs . . . Tii-gerrs' with such passion was back in the days when I had much more hair and a little less weight. And then the serious stuff I'd long dreaded began . . .

Manly's prop Mark Carroll probably didn't realise it but he helped give me an even greater sense of resolve when we packed down for the first scrum of the game and he snarled, 'You'll be off in five minutes, won't you Sirro.' 'Spud' had obviously made a note of my problems but his remark made me the more determined to try and help 'give it' to the Sea Eagles, and I found charging into their defensive line nowhere near as tough as I'd anticipated. My fitness was my only worry but whenever I felt the old energy levels start to flag I only needed to look around at the guys I was playing alongside for inspiration. Our second-rower Mark Stimson was bruising some mighty Manly reputations with his big hits; our hooker Darren Senter charged back onto the paddock moments after being carted off with a shoulder injury; the Balmain trainers had to restrain our Fijian winger James Langaloa from running back onto the field moments after he was cleaned up in a monster of a tackle by John Hopoate; and our evergreen Englishman Ellery Hanley, another ancient link to our glory days, charged into the Manly line like a prop.

And as skipper of the side, I did my best to lead by example during the sixty-five minutes I was on the paddock. We suffered a bad setback when our up-and-coming star lock Glenn Morrison was carried off the field with an ankle injury, however, testimony to the great 'eye of the Tiger' feeling about Leichhardt was the fact the poor kid came close to tears because he thought he was letting his team-mates down. It was brilliant stuff all round, and his type of commitment was appreciated by the crowd. Unfortunately, a few things went against us at crucial stages of the match and they helped Bob Fulton's Sea Eagles take the premiership points back home to Brookvale—and that hurt.

The mood in our room after the match was sombre. A few people tried to pep us up by congratulating the boys on what they called a 'gutsy effort', but we were pretty downcast. We'd had the premiers on the ropes and we'd allowed them to get back into the fight by making silly errors. It was a tough break and it was as I went over 'what could have been' when the cub reporter sidled up to me and asked me: 'Mr Sironen, what do all those years at Balmain mean to you?' As I said, it was all too much for me to grasp, and while I understood the young scribe had a job to do I heard myself stammer what must have been a painful answer for him: 'Yeah, it's been great, mate!' And I left it at that by swigging on a drink and ripping the tape from around my head.

Anyway, as I watched him walk away to check on Morrison's ankle problem I felt some regret that I hadn't given him something more than the old brush because it was the perfect opportunity to let a lot of people understand how much Balmain has meant to me over the last twelve years of my life. Hell, the Tigers had allowed me to fulfil my childhood dreams of playing not only first grade but of also representing New South Wales and Australia. As a member of Balmain I'd not only played in *two* grand finals but I had also managed to rub shoulders with some of the game's greatest players, and I made such strong friendships at Tigertown I knocked back what people called deals of a lifetime to remain with them. What did Balmain mean to me? In terms of footy it means the world to me, mate. It means the world . . .

But, I ask you, how the hell does a front-rower put those kinds of thoughts into words?

FROM SHOT-PUTTER TO TEENAGE SHOCKER

CHAPTER 2

I f it had been up to my father, Kaino, I'd have probably never known the 'joy' of being smashed in a bone-rattling tackle by the likes of David Gillespie, or the delight of scoring a try from a Steve Roach pass. Instead, I've long suspected Dad would have preferred that I represent Australia at the Olympics in either the shot-put or javelin events. The old man grew up on a farm in Finland and, like most of his mates, his childhood sporting dreams were to either play World Cup soccer or emulate the feats of Finnish Olympic heroes Villie Porhola and Jonni Myyra. They won the gold medals at the 1920 Antwerp Games for the shot-put and javelin events respectively, and while they were a bit before Dad's time, they're still revered in Finland as great champs. Many years later—and on the other side of the globe—Dad tried to instil his childhood passion for those sports into my older brother, Rod, my kid sister, Aila, and me at a time when our friends were being taught by their fathers how to play cricket and football. Mainstream Australia bracketed the 'throwing' events alongside weightlifting and wrestling as 'white wog' sports twenty years ago, but I enjoyed learning the many intricacies of what Dad called an art. I liked them because apart from seeing myself improve metre-by-metre, there was a definite

6

sense of achievement in watching Kaino nod his head in approval at our efforts. As it turned out, Dad was a bloody good coach because Aila won the NSW state under-11 and 12 shot-put titles, while I took out the zone's javelin championship and set school records for the javelin and shot-put.

My father migrated to Australia soon after he completed his national army service in 1958. As a twenty-one-year-old carpenter, he decided to leave Europe after hearing about the fantastic opportunities Australia offered anyone who was prepared to work hard. I've seen a bit of the world—admittedly, it has mainly been with the Aussie team—but I can imagine the excitement and trepidation Kaino Sironen must have felt as he farewelled his family with no more than a small suitcase and big dreams. I reckon it was a gutsy move because apart from knowing very little about the Great South Land, Dad couldn't speak a word of English! Indeed, his boat trip over was no pleasure cruise as he spent his entire time wrestling with a strange language.

Language lessons aside, the old man didn't need much time to realise he'd made the right move. He immediately fell in love with Australia's sparkling coastline and wide open spaces. As a boy who grew up near the Finnish–Russian border at the height of the Cold War, Dad has frightening memories of Soviet jet fighters flying over his family's farmhouse during tense military manoeuvres. However, in Australia he'd lobbed at a place free of not only any military threat, but it was a country burdened by few worries at all. It was a genuine paradise, and in time the land, the peacefulness and the sunny climate weren't the only things about the land of Oz Dad fell for ... yep, the big Finn lost his heart to a local girl he met at Balmoral Beach in Sydney. Her name was Blanche Davis and she was the second daughter of a police officer reputed to be as tough as old army boots. Blanche, my mother, worked as a bookkeeper for a solicitor and she was at the beach after a girlfriend insisted she meet this 'nice foreign bloke' because they'd probably get on like a house on fire. The friend was right.

Mum and Dad went out for two years before they tied the knot at St Johns Church, Willoughby, in 1961, and three products of their union are Rod, Aila and me. While it is sad to think my parents are now divorced, I can honestly say we kids were brought up in a kind and loving environment. They both worked very hard to ensure none of us went without anything, and just as importantly, they were always around if we needed their help or advice. As a matter of fact, the more I hear about the tough childhoods some kids endure, the greater I appreciate my parents' efforts to raise us right. To steal a line from Jack Gibson, they both 'done good' because our idea of a tragedy was when the rain kept us indoors for a day or two!

I first saw the light of day on 23 May 1965 when I was delivered at North Sydney's Mater Hospital and Mum still swears I made more noise on debut than the souped-up Lang Park crowd on Origin night. I can't argue with her on that score, but after having experienced the madness of an interstate battle north of the border I refuse to concede I could have dribbled like them! We were raised in the house Dad built a year before I was born in the so-called 'dress circle' of East Ryde, and to this day I maintain Finch Avenue was a brilliant place for three little Aussies to grow up. Out the back of our place was a huge bush reserve while the street teemed with kids who were happy to spend their summers playing cricket and their winters with hard-fought Rugby League Test matches.

Well, as a self-confessed boofhead you can imagine I got into my fair share of strife—and always for goofy stuff. When I was about ten my mates and I were into telephone prank calls in a *big* way. We'd dial a random number and in my deepest voice I'd ask the person at the other end of the line if Mr Wall was about? When they answered 'No', I'd demand to talk to Mrs Wall. When they replied that was also impossible, I'd gobsmack 'em with the punchline: 'Well, if there are no walls about how does your bloody house stand up?' I suppose just about every kid has used that line, but to really annoy my victims I'd laugh like a proper goose before slamming the receiver back down into the cradle. As you'd know, all good things come to an end, and the telephone calls came to an abrupt halt one afternoon when a mate phoned one of his old man's business associates. As it turned out, the joke was on us because the so-called 'sucker' recognised my friend's voice the instant he was asked whether his fridge was running. The man went along with the gag and when he replied that, yeah, it was firing on all cylinders. Well, my drongo of a mate took that as his cue to scream: 'Why aren't you out chasing it then, you idiot! It's running down the f . . . king street!' I thought it was a great hoot until a few hours later when the boy's angry mum confronted my folks to blame *me* for her son's wayward behaviour. The bloody businessman had immediately contacted my pal's father to relay an interesting tale about his fridge! Well, I copped it—and big time. Kaino was enraged by the stupidity of the calls and he ordered me to rip a switch from the willow tree in our backyard—and mate, that was always bad news. It meant a dose of old-fashioned discipline and while I realise most New Age parents aren't for punishing their kids with a clip over the ear, I'm certain the fear of copping a whack or two across the arse didn't harm any of us.

I had the typical childhood relationship with my siblings—I wanted Rod rubbed out whenever he gave me a hard time, and I know there were times when Aila hated me because I picked on her a fair bit. I especially went to town the day she returned home with her hair dyed a shocking blue colour! She was going through a rebellious stage and I don't think my smart alec comments were all that welcome. I'll never forget when Aila and her friend appeared in the newspaper dressed as punks ... Dad chucked a fit and poor Mum almost had a heart attack! However, we're good mates now and my two sons Curtis and Bayley love it when their Aunty Aila visits because she makes a great fuss over them. As for Rod, well, he gave me a hard time because like a real pest I was always trying to hang around him, but that stemmed from the secret pride I had in him. Rod was a bloody good footballer and his team-mates would bank on him to make 20 hit-ups and 30 tackles in a match, and I liked hearing the old officials in the Balmain juniors rave about him. I especially remember the day he made the Australian under-18s side in 1982 and he played along-side the likes of Dave Gillespie, Marty Bella and Brett Gale against a Papua–New Guinea side at Lang Park. It was a very proud moment for our family.

I like to think we were three good kids who kept our noses clean because the only really bad trouble I landed in at school was the morning Mr Walker, the deputy principal at East Ryde Primary, gave me four of the best for calling some girl a 'slut' at assembly. I bawled my eyes out because, apart from a pair of stinging hands, I was really confused. You see, as I had no idea what 'slut' meant, I couldn't understand why I was in strife. I knew only that the older boys said it whenever they spoke about some girls and I figured it was a term of endearment reserved for women. How dumb was that? It was a harsh lesson, and my tip for any young kid who might be reading this book is never yell 'Hello Molly, you slut!' in the playground.

Some years later, when I was sixteen, I just about broke my mother's heart when I tried grog for the first time and downed what seemed like gallons of vodka at a mate's place. A tribe of us raided his old man's liquor cabinet and while I remember thinking how awful the stuff tasted, I was determined to look cool by outdrinking my friends. So I guzzled as much as I could stomach and it didn't take long before the grog kicked in and my head started spinning and we began speaking fluent Swahili. After we finished, I lurched down my mate's driveway and his neighbour's letterbox caught my eye because it was shining under the glow of a streetlight. Thanks to the demon water I was overwhelmed by an intense desire to destroy it, and looking back on the incident now, I must've looked like the Incredible Hulk when I ripped it out from the ground with a roar. You know, it's pretty bloody funny what goes through your mind when you're young, drunk and full of testosterone. See, I have an uncle Antero back in Finland who Dad says was so strong he could lift railway sleepers above his head to win bets, and, as I swayed drunkenly in that small suburban street with some poor old lady's letterbox held high above me, I almost believed that I, Paul Sironen, was the world's strongest person. Crikey, on thinking back on that night, I realise I really was off my frigging head!

Anyhow, I didn't feel too tough when a police car responded to a Code Red that a lunatic was terrorising an entire street. I just about wet my pants when a huge copper said something about throwing the book at me for not only being drunk and disorderly, but for destroying private property. Fortunately, after a lot of fast-talking and slurred promises that it would never, ever, happen again, the sergeant let me off the hook on the proviso I apologised to the lady and repaired the damage. At the time I was so terrified of being sent to the boys' home, I'd have probably agreed to streak naked at a funeral. However, my relief to have escaped the drama seemingly scot-free turned into acute embarrassment the following morning when I returned to the lady's house. It dead-set seemed as if everyone in the street had turned out to watch the grog monster from the previous night return as a timid schoolboy—and I copped heaps. Sixteen years on I still see that bloody letterbox when I visit some old friends in the area. Occasionally, when I'm feeling nostalgic, I slow down to look at the rusting, twisted piece of metal because it is almost a monument to my one and only real night of madness as a teenager.

The year that stands out most in my childhood is definitely 1977, and for so many different reasons: *Star Wars* hit the silver screen; Australia beat the Poms by 45 runs in the Centenary Test at the Melbourne Cricket Ground; The King, Elvis Presley, died; the Queen celebrated her silver jubilee; and Paul Sironen discovered girls. Well, in a nice kind of way. I had a girlfriend named Michelle and while we did heaps of things like share popcorn at the cinema, nothing quite topped the afternoon we 'pashed off' for the first time. I can still recall nervously puckering up to her because it was to Meatloaf's album 'Paradise by the Dashboard Light', and I'm not kidding when I say I saw fireworks. Her old man came home early, and I was out the backdoor like a rocket! While the kissing was spectacular, Michelle didn't last too long—and it wasn't because of an over-protective father. Instead, she was given the big fend because, apart from having games of cricket and footy to play, I needed to remain focused to retain my status as the area's pinball wizard. It was serious stuff, and a kid established his reign as the pinny king by setting the highest score on the *Happy Days* machine in the back room of the local takeaway shop. It wasn't easy. Actually, it was quite a bloody expensive pursuit for a kid on a limited amount of pocket money. However, the old shop-owner kept us keen by promising a free barbecued chook to anyone who could beat the record score. And guess what? I won it—twice! Apart from filling my belly with juicy chunks of chook, breaking the record also helped me establish the necessary street credibility to mill about the pinny machine with all the 'cool' fellas to slurp on milkshakes, to swear, smoke illicit cigarettes and share tales (yeah, they were all lies) about girls we 'knew'.

My cigarette smoking days didn't last very long because I was at least smart enough to realise they couldn't be any good for my health or a prospective Rugby League career. However, I didn't mind sneaking the occasional beer with some mates when I was sixteen and seventeen, but it was only a 'guy's' thing. I had many buddies who dropped out of sport to dedicate their weekends to getting plastered at parties, and it was pretty sad because all they'd do was waste their Fridays and Saturdays getting pissed and trying to chat up a good sort. They thought that was the stuff of legends, but from what I could gather the best most of them ever did before turning into pumpkins after midnight was to chunder behind someone's backyard dunny. No, I wasn't tempted to follow that path because I loved my sport way too much. See, if it wasn't Rugby League, I'd play cricket for Gladesville RSL and I remember that as a happy part of my life. While two of my cricket team-mates, Paul Bevan and Paul 'Nobby' Clarke, also went on to play first grade football, I'll long remember 'Bevo' keeping wicket to mine and Nobby's express pace bowling. It was real Field of Dreams material because Nobby and I pictured ourselves as Gladesville's answer to the Aussie Test team's fast bowlers of the day, Mike Whitney and Carl Rackerman. He was Whitney because he had a massive afro, while I was Rackerman because I was tall and blond. We tried to put the fear of God into the batsmen by bowling short-pitched stuff. My greatest harvest was the day I took 8 wickets for 39 runs, and had it not been for two dropped catches (probably by Nobby) I'd have bagged all ten scalps . . . So, I thought I was pretty hot, and it was based on that and a few other Dennis Lillee-type efforts that I trialled for the Petersham Green Shield representative side. In hindsight, it is almost tragic to admit that I turned up to the trial with the hope it would be my first step towards playing a Test match against the West Indies. I say it was 'tragic' because by the end of the day my backside had been spanked red-raw by sharp-eyed batsmen who tonked my best deliveries to the boundary with very little effort. Even though I prefer to remember very few things from that game, I'm almost certain one of the batsmen who blasted me to kingdom come was Bronko Djura, who, apart from playing first grade for Souths, St George and Wests is also remembered for representing Australia in Rugby League and cricket at schoolboy level.

On the subject of school, I must confess I was never any chance of being a rocket scientist, but you'd probably have guessed as much. It was my own fault, because I didn't put much time in in hitting the books and I was also happy to play the part of the class clown. The few school reports I've kept are testimony to that because they're filled with such comments as 'Paul could do a lot better if he'd keep his mouth shut'—and the sad thing is, that ranks as one of the more positive remarks! Indeed, if they based a character in the television soap opera *Heartbreak High* on my classroom antics, he'd be the smart alec at the back of the room with a swag of stupid answers to sensible questions. For instance, if the history teacher wanted to know how the English authorities got rid of the rats that spread the plague in the fifteenth century, I'd yell out, 'They hired the Pied Piper!' Or if the science teacher asked for the difference between a kangaroo and a wallaby, I'd answer one played Rugby League and the other Rugby Union! As an adult I can now only sympathise with my old teachers because, at best, my only scholastic achievement was I constantly disrupted their classes.

I spent four years at Malvina High, but I nagged at Mum and Dad to enrol me in the prestigious Holy Cross Catholic School at Ryde which was considered one of Australia's best schoolboy football sides. I figured the exposure I could gain from playing for them in the televised schoolboy competition, the Commonwealth Bank Cup, would be invaluable for my budding football career. You see, those games were, and still are, watched by all the premiership clubs' chief executives and their lieutenants. The games are viewed as one avenue to identify fresh talent. So I wanted in, and as luck had it I was accepted to finish my final two years at Holy Cross. I knew from my first day there that I was definitely in my element: the football was taken so deadly serious by such calibre people as Ron Palmer, who now works as Phil Gould's offsider at Sydney City.

While the change of schools did wonders for my football, it didn't improve my scholastic ability one bit. Again, it was my fault— I was the boofhead who did the minimal amount of homework in between watching television or training for football. However, I wasn't a total dunce. I was pretty good at geography and I loved English because the creative writing gave me an opportunity to baffle the markers with top quality bullshit! Cripes, I even won an award at school for my efforts in Two Unit General English— students still refer to it as 'vegie' English because it is so basic— and that was because I had a slightly better grasp of the lingo than the immigrant kids I shared the classroom with!

While Mum and Dad didn't push any of us into sport, Kaino steered the three of us towards an active lifestyle. Apart from his shot-put and hammer classes, he'd also take us on 6 kilometre runs through the bush after school. In his youth, Dad was a cross-country skiing champ and he's maintained his fitness to such an extent he's still running half-marathons at sixty. He enjoyed pushing us back then, and God knows those bush-bashes were real adventures. The old man would carry a loaded spear gun to protect us from the poisonous snakes that lived in the rocks and leaves. While the runs were tough enough without the threat of being attacked by vipers, I didn't ever complain because even from an early age I realised every step and every drop of sweat was helping me build the foundations for a football career.

CHILDHOOD DREAMS

CHAPTER 3

I 've copped my fair share of boardroom backhanders during my career, but nothing floored me quite like the time in 1982 when I was overlooked by the Australian Schoolboy selectors to tour New Zealand as a prop. Perhaps it was a case of the first cut being the deepest, but fifteen years after the event I still get riled when I talk about it. I get annoyed because plenty of people told me throughout the course of the Schoolboy selection carnival that I was good enough to make the side. Despite their confidence, when the time came for the boys to pack their bags for the flight to New Zealand I was on the school bus with a packed lunch. While I've never learned why the selectors shunned me, I've long suspected I was cast aside as a result of trade-offs for particular positions. My team, the Combined Catholic Schools, won the tournament and when the 'heads' got together they picked something like ten of my team-mates. Perhaps the lobbying by the representatives from the other schools was too intense to allow an eleventh Catholic player on the Trans-Tasman flight. What added extra sting to my wounds was the fact that one prop who went with them was a member of a rag-tag team called 'The Rest'. That hurt, because that team was only there to help make up the numbers. The Rest, you see, was a mish-mash of players thrown together after they missed selection for the combined Catholics, the independent or state schools or the country team. However, when the selectors finished their Chinese meal and named the seventeen-man squad, one of them had beaten me for a start.

I have no personal gripe with the player; it was great for him and I don't want to tarnish an achievement he should still be very proud of. I was just down in the dumps because I was forced to ask myself for the very first time as a kid whether I was really any good. A few doubts entered my head, and I wondered how the hell I could ever hope to fulfil my dream of representing Australia at senior level if I couldn't make the Schoolboy side. I wallowed in self-pity for a day or two, but I snapped out of it by vowing to make the '83 team. I adopted the attitude that heaven would need to help anyone who tried to get in the way of my achieving that goal, and, for any kid who may suffer a similar setback, my advice is a get-up-and-fight attitude is much more healthy than moping about like a whipped dog.

I wasn't the only kid hurting. A fresh-faced half-back from Penrith named Greg Alexander, another member of the Catholic team, was also left behind after losing out to my good friend Scott Gale. However, I understood what he meant in his biography, *Five Star Brandy*, when Greg admitted he went home howling at the injustice of his non-selection. His frustration was understandable, as in our trial matches Greg had been the starting half-back and Scott was on the reserve bench. However, in the selection tournament Brandy was inexplicably relegated to the bench and Scott was given his chance to impress the selectors. It's funny, but fifteen years on I empathised with Brandy when I read of his heartache when he wrote: 'I was really howling at the injustice that I reckoned had been done to me, and Mum and my sisters were hugging me and trying to convince me it wasn't the end of the world.'

There were similar scenes at the Sironen household at East Ryde as Aila and Rod tried their best to comfort me. As for poor Mum and Dad, I drove them around the bend on the trip home by bawling my eyes out and going through numerous conspiracy theories! But I guess it says a lot for the prestige of the Australian Schoolboys jumper that Brandy and I felt so devastated to be left out in 1982. Indeed, in the aftermath of the ARL–Super League war, the Aussie Schoolboys side remains as one of Rugby League's great success stories. The inaugural team—the legends of '72—set an amazingly high standard by going through their tour of Great Britain undefeated. Indeed, it's almost mindblowing to think that up until 1982 no nation had been able to beat the Schoolboys from Down Under—and that was a point Phillip Street rammed home whenever they mentioned the value of supporting the Schoolboy program. Even today, a quarter of a century since that first tour, the Schoolboys are still recognised as a worthwhile project because some great players who have come through the system include internationals Les Boyd, Craig Young, Royce Ayliffe, Paul Langmack, Andrew Ettingshausen, Steve Menzies, Benny Elias and Andrew Farrar.

However, the '82 Schoolboys made newspaper headlines and radio news bulletins on the afternoon an Auckland schoolboy side defeated them. It was the first time the Aussies had ever tasted defeat and if I'm going to be totally honest, I should admit a slight grin came to my face on hearing the news . . . but it was through jealousy, not malice. These days when I look back on the trial and trepidation of '82 I still feel dirty about my treatment, but being a little more mature (just a bit) I like to think the experience was a test to see if I'd bounce back. It was almost as if life had turned around and said, 'Righto mate, you've had a good run, but let's see how fair dinkum you really are!' Well, I was bloody fair dinkum and I trained even harder; I asked my coaches more probing questions and I set myself higher personal standards. It was tough, and sometimes I played four games a week because of obligations to my school, the North Ryde club, the Combined Catholic College side and the Tigers' junior representative side. And all the hard yakka paid off when I made the 1983 Australian Schoolboys Merit side.

As a result of the low point of '82 and all the extra work I put in, I rate my being named in the '83 team as perhaps *the* most rewarding moment of my teenage years. The drive home from Newcastle the second time around was a lot happier. Rather than shedding tears of despair, the family spilt tears of joy—and our handkerchief was a beaut extra-large green and gold jumper! Regrettably, I didn't wear that jersey into battle because we didn't have any opposition to play in '83, but it sits proudly among my most prized possessions all the same. I'm happy to report Brandy also enjoyed better fortune that year. He took the No. 7 jumper home to Penrith, and I'm sure that acknowledgment helped spur him along to what has been a magnificent career.

I've already admitted a babe named Michelle was my first girlfriend when I was twelve, but make no bones about it, Rugby League vied with the police force as the first real love of my life. I can vividly recall my introduction to the game. I was thrown on as a prop to help make up the numbers for the Gladesville Bowling and Sports Club when I was just six years old. I'd spent the night over at a friend's place and when his parents took him to the local park his team was short a player so they conscripted me. I had no idea of what was happening, but they gave me a jumper and the instructions to go out and enjoy myself . . . and I did. I don't think my team-mates were too impressed by my idea of fun, however, because I not only helped the opposition drag them to the ground whenever they had the ball, but I ran backwards the few times I managed to catch the pigskin in an effort not to be tackled. And it gets better—I can even recall sitting down to make mud pies at one stage of the game. It was perhaps the worst ever debut in the history of junior football, but I'd been blooded and I was hooked . . . at just six years of age I knew Rugby League would have a huge bearing on my life.

In my first season I won Gladesville's Most Improved Player award and in time it became a battle between me and the future Olympic runner Darren Clarke to see who bagged the most tries each season. Darren was quick and deceptive, I was big and mobile, and together we formed a handy partnership to score 40 or 50 tries a season. I spent six happy winters with Gladesville, but at thirteen, I sprouted a few inches and I started having problems with my knees. I still don't know for certain whether they were just growing pains but it was sometimes hard to walk, let alone run. My parents figured it would be best if I didn't play football for a year and I was happy to toe the line, but I was bored and I started to climb the wall through the sheer frustration of being sidelined. Around April I received a call from Gladesville's arch rivals, North Ryde, and I decided to bite the bullet and play footy.

I was a funny kid because I ran everywhere. I'd run to the shop; to school if I missed the bus; to my mate's place; along bush tracks with Dad; and I'd even run the 9 kilometre round trip from my place to North Ryde's home ground on Old Kent Road for training when I was fourteen. Hell, I ran so often I could've probably given

Tom Hanks's alter ego Forest Gump a run for his money during his epic trip across America. But my extra fitness paid off because I played some junior representative football for the Central Metropolitan team, and when I turned twelve I was given my first state jumper for NSW Primary Schools in a match against Queensland. The thrill of running out onto the hallowed Sydney Cricket Ground wasn't lost on me when we played the curtain-raiser to the NSW–Great Britain match in 1977, but I really don't remember too much about the game except the Canetoads were hard little bastards who got off on thumping anyone in a blue jumper. I can also remember two guys who trialled for the NSW team—Ian Roberts and Glenn Lazarus. Roberts was a flashy player even back then because he was lean 'n' fit and had plenty of courage. Lazzo, on the other hand, was a roly-poly sort of a kid who looked as though he should have been at home watching the footy on television while devouring bowls of popcorn and chips. Don't get me wrong, Glenn was a more than handy player—he just didn't look like your typical schoolboy footy star because he carried a bit of puppy fat about. While Triple-J radio stars Roy Slaven and HG Nelson were to christen him the 'Brick with Eyes' in later life, Glenn was more your 'Sponge with Eyes' back then. Anyway, it's almost crazy to think the three of us toured Great Britain and France on the historic 1994 Kangaroo tour, isn't it?

My most memorable football trip as a kid was when Balmain's under-12 rep side toured New Zealand to take on some 'baby' Maoris who were built like mini-Mac trucks. We were based at a place called Mangere East, near Auckland, and I don't know what's in the water over there because they weren't just big kids—they were bloody monsters who knew how to crunch an opponent with hard tackles. They cleaned me up a few times, but they had trouble catching Darren Clarke because he moved like a gazelle even way back then. In New Zealand, however, I'm certain he was motivated by fear, and fear alone. The other reason for the trip across the Tasman, to gain a broader outlook on life by meeting people in a different country, was also beneficial for me because I was billeted with the Rack family. They were very generous people who made sure I enjoyed my stay in New Zealand by taking me on a three-day sailing trip around the spectacular Bay of Islands. It was tremendous, and one of my fondest memories from that sojourn was hooking a 9 pound snapper and gorging myself on it at

dinnertime. Yeah, I loved my tucker even way back then. The Racks'
hospitality had such an impact on my childhood that I broke camp
when the 1993 Aussie team was in New Zealand to catch up with
them.

When I was sixteen my brother Rod was graded with the Tigers
and seeing him mix with local heroes such as Wayne Pearce and
David Brooks spurred me on. Thankfully, Rod didn't mind fuelling
my fire because he'd occasionally take me along to the Leagues
Club gym to train and it was there, among the dumbbells and
running machines, I first met 'Junior' Pearce. The guy was a Trojan,
and I could only shake my head in disbelief as he'd push himself
beyond the normal limits. Indeed, I realised there and then he was
the prototype forward for the modern game and that I'd need to
follow his tough standards if I wanted to make it.

My first step was to serve my apprenticeship in the Tigers'
junior representative teams and an important part of my Rugby
League education came in an SG Ball match against the Penrith
Panthers. For those of you who don't know, Penrith is a tough place
where men are men and the women are grateful for it . . . well,
sometimes. But none of us appreciated the day we arrived at the
Panthers 'snake pit' to find we were playing guys with goatee beards,
hairy chests and an obvious penchant for rough-house tactics! As a
matter of fact, when you'd come across kids from the other rep
teams such as Manly or Cronulla, they'd offer a word of warning
about Penrith and Wests. I thought they were joking when they
warned that blokes from those two teams would rip your balls off,
but they weren't. One Penrith bludger brought tears of pain to my
eyes when he executed an evil 'Christmas hold'. I squealed like a
stuck pig. Crikey, the pain was so bad I even looked down my shorts
just to make sure my crown jewels were still in their rightful place—
much to the mirth of everyone else!

However, my halo slipped during a Jersey Flegg game against St
George in 1983 when I made what was a terrible spear tackle on a
Dragon forward. It was dreadful, and when I saw what I'd done on
a video replay a few nights later I squirmed in my seat. Unfortunately,
the player's momentum helped me lift him 6 feet in the air and I
drove him head first into the ground so hard he hit the turf with a
loud thud. I just about shat my pants as he lay motionless at my
feet because I thought I'd broken his neck. It was a terrifying few
moments, and unfortunately I didn't see the fellow get up and walk

off for treatment because I was busy swapping punches with a few of his mates who wanted to extract some revenge. When the referee finally restored order I was promptly dispatched to the sin bin. I sat there feeling like the biggest bully since Brutus thumped Popeye, and after the game my father told me to never, *ever* do that again— the boy was lucky not to be in a wheelchair. Dad was right, and since that incident I'm totally against the spear tackle—it is fraught with danger. One of the Phillip Street initiatives I've applauded over the years is their hard line on that brand of a tackle. I believe anyone who fronts the judiciary for 'spearing' an opponent deserves the maximum suspension.

Despite that controversy, I was granted a $500 scholarship with the Tigers and I blew the cheque on a state-of-the-art stereo. Every afternoon after school before running off to training I'd pump up the volume and play all my favourite hits from Elton John, Dragon and SuperTramp. However, I learned the hard way that even money can't guarantee a player protection from injuries because, not long after being given my scholarship, I tore my calf muscle in the SG Ball semi-final and it ended my season. Not only was I forced to sit on the sideline and watch Greg Alexander spearhead Penrith to a grand final win over us, but the injury also cost me a possible trip to New Zealand with the Northern Suburbs Schoolboy Rugby Union. I went along to the trial with a few schoolmates from Malvina High and trialled as a *fullback*! And, I reckon I was more than half a chance of going because I scooted away for a 90 metre try—and that's no word of a lie!

While I may have missed the Australian Schoolboy tour in '82, one of my most treasured memories from my junior days occurred earlier that year when the Tigers beat a star-studded Cronulla Sharks outfit for the Jersey Flegg title at the old Sydney Sports Ground. It was a huge buzz and when I thumb through the old program and see Cronulla was stacked with such future top guns as Andrew Ettingshausen, Mark McGaw, Jonathon Docking, Barry Russell and Stuart Raper it reinforces my belief that it really was a grand achievement. I don't know what it was about the Balmain junior rep teams back in the early to mid-1980s, but we were always in the thick of the action despite being a tiny junior competition. I guess we personified the old saying about performance, and not size, being the most important issue. However, the Tigers boasted such hard guys as Paul Clarke, Ron Ryan, Jamie Davidson and Paul

Bevan back then, and their toughness brought the whiz-kids back a couple of pegs. Nowadays, the Balmain juniors are struggling and I reckon its all about demographics ... There just aren't as many kids living in the area since the trendies moved in and converted homes that once housed families of six or seven kids into art studios or inner-city bachelor apartments. It's a crying shame that my first team, the Gladesville Bowling and Recreation club, can't even field a Rugby League side now because the kids aren't there for them. It's a pity because I think junior football is character building and it certainly steels children to handle tough situations as they get older. Indeed, one of the brightest memories I have from playing football as a kid is of the many wonderful people I came across. I've no doubt my old coaches and managers had a positive influence on most of my team-mates and me. I'm certain that if nothing else, their willingness to take an interest in a bunch of kids helped us grow to be better people.

DOWN AND OUT IN WAIKIKI

CHAPTER 4

The day I knew I *really* wanted to make my mark in Rugby League was in 1984 and I was lying on Waikikii Beach in Hawaii. I was watching the waves lapping on the American shores, and I thought of them leaving Bondi on the other side of the globe and I wanted to be there. I'd been in America for five months and learning the many intracacies of gridiron at the University of Hawaii and I was homesick ... I longed for Sydney and I wanted to play Rugby League. League, not gridiron, was in my heart, and it had been that way ever since I was a kid of seven, but I maintain my stint in Hawaii with the University of Hawaii Rainbows gave my Rugby League career one hell of a leg-up.

I was granted a full scholarship with the Rainbows when an official involved with the 1983 Australian Schoolboys side sent a video of me in action to Hawaii's head defensive coach, Rich Ellison. Ellison saw some potential and three months after I finished Year 12 I was on a Boeing 747 to live what many people would call a dream. The things I learned there were fantastic, and when I say the University of Hawaii opened a whole new world for me I'm not talking about gaining an appreciation for American literature or political science! No, the insights I obtained for such things as sports science, diet and nutrition were unbelievable. And then there were the gym facilities—mate, they were mind-blowing. When I walked into the uni's gymnasium for the first time, I thought it was the set for a sci-fi movie. There were flashing lights, beeping sounds, bright buttons and machines made out of white tubular metal. Indeed, the set-up was so modern there are still some Rugby League clubs that lack the equipment that university boasted thirteen years ago.

And I got acquainted with almost every one of those machines because part of my initiation to college football was to hit the weights in four tough sessions a week. It was a rude awakening—the most I'd ever lifted in Sydney was 80 kilos—but the American trainers kept stacking extra lumps of metal on my bar until I was heaving 145 kilos. And the results were amazing! By the end of my Hawaiian stint I'd whacked on 10 kilos of muscle and improved my strength and speed. To this day I'm certain the intense gym work I did in Honolulu helped me break into first grade at Balmain a season or two before my time.

It was also from spending time over there that I developed a healthy respect for American football and the blokes who play it. It is because of that respect I refute the common perception in Australia that American footballers are 'pussies' because they wear protective padding and helmets. Instead, I consider them to be very fit and hard guys who are in a cut-throat sport. In saying that though, I don't believe American footballers have the overall stamina of our blokes. While a League forward is expected to perform for 80 minutes, the big Americans are only out on the field for a few, explosive moments. As much as I enjoy watching it, I do think the American game is a little bit too programed—everything has to be so precise there isn't much room for the type of spontaneity that makes Rugby League and even AFL an exciting spectacle. But I appreciate aspects of the sport such as the big hits, the catching skill of a running back and the intelligence of a quarterback. I religiously watch the NFL action on television, and occasionally my thoughts drift back to my days as a 'Red Shirt' with the Rainbows, who compete in the Western Athletic Conference.

A Red Shirt is someone who takes a compulsory season off from playing. See, a player in the American college system is 'signed' to a five-year deal, but he's obliged to sit one of the years out to recover from any injuries and, I suppose, to allow himself some time to focus on his studies. Because I arrived in Honolulu ignorant of even the most basic of gridiron skills, the hierarchy decided to make my first year a Red Shirt and I learned things like the calls, the drills and the techniques in earnest. It was tough going; even getting dressed for battle was an education. See, you have all these protective items to put on and their combined weight is 12 kilos. Lord knows I'll never forget the humiliation I felt when I walked in on my first team meeting wearing the butt protector over my old fella. All my new team-mates cracked up and an Afro-American guy added to my embarrassment when he laughed, 'Man, if your penis is *that* laaaaarge you must be a brother painted white!'

Well, if wrestling with the hazards of dressing wasn't enough, I also had to contend with the American coaches who demand military-like regimentation. For instance, if a player was late for training or forgot his helmet they'd unleash the wrath of hell upon him. I was always under extra pressure to perform because I was over there on a full scholarship despite the fact I didn't know the first thing about gridiron. So the college expected excellence, and apart from scrutinizing the efforts on the training paddock the heads also kept a close eye on my scholastic ability. Thankfully, the classes weren't that hard. For instance, in Arts 101 (American literature) I just had to read *The Great Gatsby* in my first semester . . . it was a snack! What made it tough, however, was the time I had to spend on other things. My daily timetable went something like: two classes before lunch, one class after lunch, start training at 3 pm, complete training at 7 pm, eat dinner, relax and study.

Although my scholarship involved some hard yakka, there was definitely a lot of hype and bullshit about it. For instance, even though I was only a Red Shirt I still had to get decked in all the playing gear on match day and charge out with the starting line-up. It was full-on American razzamatazz and in the bleachers there'd be 50 000 fans screaming their heads off. Some of the best-looking cheer girls you could ever hope to see strutted their stuff while the university's brass band would get the whole joint jumping by belting out the theme song from the TV series *Hawaii Five-O*. Just to sit on the bench was an amazing experience—the atmosphere was akin to a State of Origin match. It was a buzz. I really regret not ever getting the chance to play in a game. If I could have played I'd have wanted it to be the one the Balmain boys attended when they lobbed into Hawaii for their end of season trip. They turned up at the stadium expecting to see me 'sack' (tackle) the quarterback, yet all they saw was me charge out onto the field in all my armour and go through the stretching and prematch drills before taking my spot in the bleachers, where I'd high five any good moves with the other Red Shirts. The boys laughed themselves silly and as the game progressed I squirmed uneasily as a couple of them yelled to the coach, 'Put Sirro on' and 'Give Sirro a go, ya mug!' With each chant of 'We want Sirro' I turned a deeper shade of red, though I couldn't help laughing that night when Junior, Blocker, Benny, my brother Rod and the other boys gave it to me when we hit what the Americans like to call 'brewskis'. I copped, 'Good game mate, man-of-the-match-stuff'. 'You must be exhausted after all that work', 'Did you get hurt out there?'

I shared a room for my first month in Honolulu with a volleyballer from Santa Barbara named Peter Parker. He was your typical Californian guy who didn't take life overly serious. Hell, Pete Parker didn't even worry about my loud snoring or the occasional nights when I'd roll home full of ink. While there I was lucky to have an Aussie legend named Colin Scotts take me under his wing. The former Australian Rugby Union Schoolboys star had been in Hawaii since 1982 and he had the place cased. At 125 kilos and 2 metres, he could walk into any bar and everyone would know who he was. After he finished college Colin became personal friends with Sammy Davis Jnr, the girls thought he was gorgeous and the barmen plied him with free drinks. Heck, the guy's popularity was so high a traffic cop said he'd let Colin off a fine if he'd sign an autograph! Back home he came from a very successful family based on Sydney's northern beaches. His old man made a bit of money as a property developer while one of his sisters is the renowned fashion designer Wendy Heather. With such a background you'd suspect Colin was born with a silver spoon in his mouth, but, take it from me, he's one tough cookie. I heard about the crap he went through when he first arrived in Hawaii and I reckon it took a lot of courage for him to see it out. See, the Americans loathed him . . . they saw him as an outsider taking a full scholarship away from one of their own and they treated him with utter contempt. The guys he played with heckled him, they belittled him and I'm told a few even spat on him. But Colin didn't back down, he just looked 'em in the eye and said, 'Come on, give me your best shot!' Because Colin proved Australians were good enough to be of NFL standard, he made it easier for guys like me to be more easily accepted.

I was soon in an off-campus condo with Colin, Ray Ljubisic (a bear-like Canadian) and a huge Kiwi named Craig Ormsby. I was the baby of the unit and they did their best to corrupt me . . . and they succeeded. There were some wild nights there . . . and I pitied our neighbours when some of our shindigs dragged on into the early hours of the morning and they didn't dare knock on our door because they were put off by the sheer size and bulk of us! Above all, Colin proved to be a tremendous—and understanding—mate. He realised as a kid on a scholarship I was doing it very tough for finances over there. I was on $US200 a month, but to enjoy a single decent night out on the town in Honolulu you needed about $US100 (probably $US175 now) and it was only through his generosity that I sampled the great nightlife Hawaii has to offer. He was a legend, and I don't think I've ever known a bloke who could win the girls over like him. I'll never forget the time we returned from a holiday on the US mainland a few days before school opened and we were stranded for accommodation. I thought we'd have to sleep on the beach, but Colin solved our problems by slicking his hair back, and putting on a cool-looking shirt and cruising the five star hotels. He chatted up a wealthy-looking boiler who could have walked off the set of *Dallas* or even *Melrose Place* and he had her eating out of his hands. Within half an hour he'd arranged for us to act as her bodyguards! We were given the presidential suite, but I was the bloke who slept the three nights on the hallway floor.

Colin used to like to tell the American media when he played for the Pheonix Cardinals that he was a 'character', and I wouldn't dispute that. Whenever he'd make a 'sack' he'd celebrate by performing a Kangaroo hop, and he did a few other things to enhance his reputation as the 'Crocodile Dundee' of the NFL. For instance, there was the time when he was off the coast of Hawaii competing in a game-fishing contest on the same boat as Joseph P. Kennedy II, the son of the late Robert Kennedy. Anyway, their fishing was interrupted by a Mayday call from a boat that was sinking in shark-infested waters. Colin and then Kennedy dived into the water to save the two survivors and after they were pulled aboard Colin returned to the rapidly sinking boat because he realised a fish was attached to one of the lines. After reeling it in they found the marlin was a 226 kilogram monster, big enough to win second place in the competition. Yeah, he was one crazy character, all right, and his favourite gee-up to the gullible Americans was that cars in Sydney had square tyres so the locals could practice their kangaroo shooting as the cars hopped along the street.

Adventures with Colin and the boys notwithstanding, I soon grew homesick and often wondered how the Balmain reserve grade side was going. I'd catch the bus to the beaches at Waikiki and ask myself, 'What the hell are you doing here, Sirro?' I'd spend hours wondering about my future, and I couldn't see American football there. Instead, I saw myself in a police uniform and a first grade football jumper. My heart just wasn't in American football and towards the end of my time there I treated the whole thing as a bit of a holiday. I took off for a while to the mainland and toured California, Nevada and Reno. It was a great time . . . I even went to Disneyland and met Mickey Mouse. When I returned to Hawaii I knew I didn't want to achieve the great American dream—an NFL contract—and I made arrangements to return and play in the lower grades at Balmain.

Before I boarded the plane home I did a bit of star-gazing and saw such celebrities as Tom Selleck, Mr T and Sylvester Stallone. Actually, Stallone turned up to one of our training sessions one afternoon to do some sprint work. It was just after he'd made *Rocky* and he was surrounded by bodyguards who looked as if they were out of *Pulp Fiction*. Despite their menacing stares, a few of us managed to scream, out, 'AADDRIIIAAANNNNNNEEE!' like Stallone's alter ego at the end of the movie. As a matter of fact, I was surprised when I saw Stallone because he was a lot smaller than I guessed he'd be. However, one woman who lived up to all expectations of size and assets was country and western star Dolly Parton. I spied her at the famous Shorebird Bar, and what can I say except she is one well-built lady! Fortunately Dolly wasn't about on my last night in Hawaii, because it was pretty ugly. After many hours of consuming as much grog as humanly possible I ended up in a hotel elevator with a few of the boys . . . we were butt-naked, swigging from bottles of spirits and we had a ghetto blaster playing the latest Dragon casette full bore. It was a bizarre ending to a bizarre, but enjoyable enough, time of my life.

At the beginning of the '97 season Balmain had a few former American footballers trialling for contracts, but for reasons unknown to me they switched to Redfern in the hope of gaining a contract with Souths. I watched them closely and it seemed to me those guys, as big and athletic as they were, were having trouble grasping the basics. I believe it comes back to what a guy is born and raised with . . . just as was the case with me in Hawaii back in 1984. I do believe there are some Americans who have the raw material to make their name in Rugby League because there is a high 'churn' rate of college stars who don't make the NFL. One guy who I recall is Kent Unterman, a Tight End player from the University of Hawaii. He was a talented athlete who could benchpress 220 kilos, he could run 100 metres in 11.1 seconds and he hit the scales at 110 kilos. If there isn't a club in the ARL or Super League competitions who wouldn't kill for a player with those attributes then I'll turn it up.

On my return to Australia I saw Paul Langmack out at an Amco Cup match and his eyes almost popped out of his head when he saw how much weight I'd gained while I was in the States. The first thing he asked was whether I'd hit the juice in between classes and training sessions at the university, and even though I denied it, word got about I'd hit the steroids. Well, it was crap, because the only thing I hit over there was the tackling bag and the weights. I didn't let the accusations get to me because I knew the truth. However, I will admit I know of some guys in Hawaii who did take steroids and I saw how the drugs altered their features . . . they started to look like cavemen! I was never offered any steroids over there and I can honestly say if anyone had suggested I tried them, they'd have copped an old-fashioned don't argue!

I finished 1984 by playing a handful of reserve grade games with Balmain and I felt like Superman because of my strength and speed. I constantly broke the line, and while in defence I banged plenty of my opponents over. It felt great and after I played Manly's reserves that year their coach Bob Fulton mentioned me in his column in the *Big League* program.

I had other things on my mind apart from football however. I'd applied to join the police force and when my papers finally came through I was given permission by the Tigers' heirarchy to miss summer training and attend the coppers' academy at Goulburn— 300-odd kilometres from Frank Stanton's whip-cracking sessions at Leichhardt.

BALMAIN BLUE HEELER

CHAPTER 5

The toughest test I faced as a police officer was the night I attended a murder at a hostel for deaf and dumb people at Glebe, a trendy suburb in Sydney's inner-city. Mine was the first squad car on the scene, and it was a horrific one . . . a young girl had been stabbed to death and her blood was everywhere. It was sickening. Instead of allowing myself to be upset I went straight into police mode and followed the textbook procedure. I interviewed the only witness—and Christ, what a witness! He was a weasely, long-haired type whose body was covered in tattoos and his earlobes were studded with a variety of earrings. His appearance wasn't the worry, however, it was his deafness that created all the problems. After a few frustrating minutes of trying to decipher his frantic sign language, I figured it would be easier if he drew the murderer. Well, his artwork astounded me, not because he was a budding Rembrandt, but the nut sketched himself! I was amazed, because I'd never have picked him as a vicious bloke. Sure, he looked *different*, but I figured he was just one of those people who go through life trying to appear tougher than they really are. Boy, wasn't I wrong. As it turned out, he was a spiteful little bastard who killed the woman when she refused to be his girlfriend—not being able to take rejection was an excuse that angered even the hardened detectives who thought they'd heard it all. The postscript to the only homicide I attended was just as dreadful: the murderer necked himself in prison . . . it was a crazy frigging set-up.

When I look back on my police career I recall four unspectacular years of foot and highway patrols, breaking up the occasional pub brawl, attending domestic disputes, performing mundane station duties and booking illegally parked motorists. I have a swag of friends who religiously watch the action-packed police shows on television and they're always asking me to recall my accounts of high-speed chases, shoot-outs and daring drug busts. Well, they're wasting their time—I saw about as much action as an old-aged pensioner in a bingo hall. Not that I'm complaining—if I could have somehow winged it, I'd have been stationed in the kitchenette on tea-and-toast duty whenever the dangerous jobs were assigned.

Despite my inclination for the quiet life, I drew my service revolver the night a gang of armed robbers raided the Leichhardt MarketTown. A mob of us were sent there to help the Tactical Response Group search the area and I fair dinkum just about pooped my pants. While the TRG guys were in their element and howling like wolves at the moon, I was terrified a psycho with nothing to lose would bob up from nowhere and start firing at me. It was a bastard of a feeling and I'll always remember thinking as we ran from door to door looking for the gunmen that my $32 000 a year police salary wasn't enough to risk a bullet for. Fortunately, I escaped that awful experience unscathed and you can rest assured I was always in the kitchenette and guarding the kettle whenever the inspector yelled for volunteers.

When I quit the force in 1990 I was roasted by my colleagues for what they called a piss-poor arrest record—two arrests in four years. What they overlooked was the amount of parking tickets I wrote. Mine was a sterling effort, and I even reckon the Premier should have presented me with a medal for suffering writer's cramp in the line of duty. The biggest blue I made as a parking cop was the evening I mistakenly booked my sister-in-law's cousin, Grant 'The Lizard' Regan. I didn't know it was his car illegally parked in the No Standing Zone, but he realised by the signature on his ticket that I was responsible for his hefty fine and he went ballistic . . . even 'Blocker' Roach's famous onfield dummy spits paled in comparison. Actually, now I think of it, I should have also nabbed The Lizard for offensive language—that would have *really* fixed him.

You can probably gather I wasn't the best officer to have ever walked the beat, but there were few prouder probationary constables than me when Class 216 graduated from the Goulburn Police Academy in 1986. It signalled the finale to three tough months of doing such drills as baton-work and general policing, but funnily enough, marching gave me my most trouble. I reckon the fact an instructor dubbed me 'Two-left-feet' Sironen best sums up my parade ground blues. Nevertheless, there was a definite spring in my step—albeit Gomer Pyle-style—the day we graduated. I was over the moon because I'd fulfilled my childhood dream to follow the heavy footsteps left by my grandfather Ivan 'Porky' Davis. Even though Pop died when I was only seven I was enthralled by the stories my grandmother told me about his thirty-eight years in the service. Indeed, it is still a great source of family pride that the infamous underworld figure Darcy Dugan didn't escape from Sydney's Central lockup when Grandpop was on duty—and history notes that was no mean feat! Dugan was originally sentenced to death in 1950 for his part in the hold-up shooting of a Sydney bank manager, but when that was overturned to life imprisonment he developed into an escape artist who could've even taught the great Harry Houdini a trick or two. He broke out of jail with such an annoying frequency, 'doing a Darcy Dugan' became colloquial language for an unlikely escape from police custody—but never when Porky Davis was on duty.

I enjoyed the camaraderie of the police station because it was an extension of the Tigers' great team spirit. It was one-in, all-in, which is to be expected as a cop needs to be able to depend on his partner in what could easily be a life-or-death situation. And coppers really do look after a mate who is doing it tough. I found the most commonly used remedy for any problem, from a bad case to a personal drama, was a HUUUUUGE night at the pub, and for the main it helped let off loads of steam. And, there were times when I saw beefy sergeants drop their guard and offer a few kind words to a colleague who was having a rough time and, believe me, any recipient would value those words like gold because it was a mighty effort for some sergeants to even wish you a happy birthday.

As for me, I realised early in the piece to switch off emotionally from the many traumas of the job because I knew it would be disastrous to fall into the trap of getting attached to a case, such as that girl's murder in Glebe. That didn't mean I didn't care, I just realised it was the best thing for sanity's sake.

There were, of course, some funny times and I copped heaps after the state government dropped the height restriction which once kept gnomes out of the force because I was buddied up with a bloke who was 5 foot 4 inches in elevator shoes! It was hilarious, and I'm sure Laurel and Hardy didn't get as many laughs as my little mate and I received whenever we walked the beat around Leichhardt. It was comical because he was so short. I had little old ladies tug at my sleeve to say sparks were coming from off his baton as it dragged along the pavement! Unfortunately his shortness was a big problem for him, and a few times he suggested I should walk in the gutter to make him look taller! While there was no way I would ever have agreed to that, I used to enjoy patrolling with him because anything could happen. I reckon there have been a few jokes based on this character and his experiences, like the early morning we caught an elderly drunk driver who was going the wrong direction in a one way street. 'Sir, you're drunk!' said my partner in disgust. The old bloke made me piss myself when he fired back, 'Son, you're jealous!' My little buddy wasn't going to let him get the better of him and he said, 'Sir, you are intoxicated, and as a result you aren't in proper control of the car. Your vehicle was weaving all over the street when we pulled you over!' Strangely, a look of relief came over the old codger's face and he laughed, 'Thank goodness, I thought my steering was stuffed.' By now the steam was coming out of my partner's ears and nostrils and he yelled, 'Sir, you're also driving up a one way street. What the hell is going on?' To that the old boy shrugged his shoulders, puffed on a smoke, and said; 'Mate, I don't know, but it can't be that good because every bastard is coming back!'

I did the rounds of Eighth Division, the police district that takes in Annandale, Glebe, Balmain and Leichhardt, and I met some top blokes along the way. One of the cheeriest was the crown sergeant at Balmain, Jack Newton Snr, whose son is considered one of Australia's best ever golfers. Newton had been in the force for donkey's years and when I met him I figured he'd *forgotten* more about police work than most officers would hope to learn in a lifetime. However, the greatest lesson he taught me had nothing to do with law enforcement, but golf. We were out on the course one day and I was playing a shocker ... when I wasn't playing the ball into the woods it was landing in the sand bunker and it even reached the stage when I seriously considered throwing my putter in the lake. Anyway, big Jack told me if I wanted to whittle my handicap down I just needed to slow my swing down—and while I don't lay claim to being a threat to Greg Norman, Jack's tip helped.

Some of the best lessons a young police officer can gain come from being thrown in the deep end and fending for themselves. For instance, I used to dread prison van duty—hell, I'd have even preferred to take on Rugby League tough guys 'Rambo' Ronny Gibbs and Les 'Bundy' Davidson on the footy field any day. See, whenever convicted criminals are sent from the courthouse to Long Bay Jail, they have a young police officer accompany them in the back of the van. I loathed it—not because I felt threatened, but because I knew I'd cop heaps when they'd decide to blame the walloper for their fate and give him a gobful. God knows I could fill a book with the insults I fielded from some heavy duty dudes who recognised my melon from the sports pages. They'd snarl things like, 'You're a dog Sironen. My grandmother tackles harder than you' or 'I didn't know they let police poofters play football'. I'd normally agree that by the look of them their grandmother probably *could* tackle harder than me, but I'd also offer them the sound advice not to bend over in the showers when they dropped the soap. Not all the prisoners wanted to bag me—hell, some even wanted to talk about footy on their way to serving their time. I even had this one guy ask me to sign an autograph for 'Ken'. When I asked whether Ken was his son, the fella shook his head and said, 'Nah mate, me alias!'

I pulled quite a lot of shifts at the Coroner's Court and sitting with the stiffs was definitely a lot more peaceful than the prison van. The hours were great for my footy training commitments but, take it from me, the hours were about the only civilised aspect of the job. It was in the morgue's freezers where I learned what they mean by 'man's inhumanity to man', because I saw corpses that had been mutilated, old people who'd been bashed to death and even the remains of people who'd been the victims of random rapes and murders. Believe me, it is a sick world out there, and simply reading the court briefs of the cases that were to be heard that day was enough to make my skin crawl. The forensic scientists who worked at the morgue were also a different breed from anyone I'd ever met before—Steve Roach and Sam Backo included. I got along pretty well with one bloke and I fielded an urgent call from him one morning when he needed some help to identify something that had lobbed on his desk—well, so he said. It was a bad geez up, because when I entered his room looking me square in the eye was a severed head that had been floating in a river for three months. I won't go into the gruesome details but it's suffice to say it was a frigging battle to keep my breakfast down.

One of my other duties at the Coroner's Court was to guard the prisoners in their cells and while a few of them had interesting yarns to spin the bloke who had the biggest impact on me was a hitman named Franciscus 'Bill' Vandenberg. He was the most unlikeliest murderer you could ever have met—he was mild-mannered, into art and, most of all, Vandenberg acknowledged he'd done the wrong thing. He was charged with the contract murder of hotelier's wife Megan Kalajzich as she slept next to her husband in the family home, and the case received widespread media attention. As the trial unravelled, Vandenberg emerged as a hardworking and community-spirited man who was overwhelmed by financial problems. I don't believe there are any reasons that justify a murder, and money is at the bottom of the list, and that was something Vandenberg realised when it was too late. He was terribly sorry for what he'd done and it didn't surprise me to later learn prison officers with twenty-years' experience had never come across a convict with his depth of remorse. Vandenberg was in a state of mental hell because he couldn't live with the fact that he not only had blood on his hands, but he'd also destroyed the lives of the Kalajzich family and shamed his own. Two years after our meeting I read Vandenberg killed himself and I guess it didn't surprise me all that much. I'd gathered from our conversations he was a man living in total agony. Whenever I happen to think of Vandenberg I consider his a story everyone should heed when they think about taking any short cut in life.

After four years in the service I found it was too tough a juggling act to combine my police workload with my ever-increasing Rugby League commitments. The duty roster was my worst enemy because some of my shifts during the footy season were absolute shockers. Many of my colleagues swapped their shifts to help me prepare properly for a big game and while I'll always be grateful for their generosity, there were times when I couldn't avoid the dreaded graveyard gig and I'd be on patrol from midnight to dawn. And, as you could imagine, there were times when I had to drag myself from the Tigers dressing room after a tough match against the likes of Manly and Canberra to ride shotgun in a patrol car. Sometimes I'd turn up to work looking like the victim of a gang war, but I had no choice in the matter . . . it would have been poor form to leave a colleague carrying the can back at the station. The only time I resented being on duty was two days after the '89 grand final loss because while I was behind the cop shop counter and filing reports on lost pets, my buddies were back on the tiles at the pub and going through all the post mortems for our heartbreaking loss to Canberra. It certainly wasn't the way I'd have planned it.

I wasn't the only footballer leading such a tough schedule back in 1986, however. There were eighteen policemen playing first grade, and some of them were great talents: Phil Daley and Mal Cochrane at Manly, Craig Young and Paul Osborne at St George, and Donny McKinnon at Norths. I'm certain there were times when they too were tired of the tough shifts and other demands of the job, but it certainly didn't hinder their careers. Daley, McKinnon and Young represented Australia, Cochrane won the Rothmans Medal in '86 and Osborne established himself as one of the game's great ball distributors. Actually, whenever I thought I was doing it tough on the beat, I used to spare a thought for 'Ossie' Osborne who was based at Newtown, an inner-city suburb that boasts more than one gay venue. Perhaps the funniest story I heard was how Osborne, a very happy and red-blooded heterosexual, went undercover in a sleazy gay bar to serve a summons on a wanted person. Now, legend has it that big beefy Ossie waited a few minutes before he followed the bloke into the toilets to serve him the summons, but when he entered the Gents the toilet cubicle was locked. Ossie knocked on the door and asked if 'Joe Bloggs' was in there. Well, you can imagine the front-rower's shock when an effeminate male voice lisped in reply, 'Yeth it ith, big boy. Come in!'

Ultimately, I found the grind of serving two masters, Rugby League and the police force, too demanding as my annual leave was being chewed up by such football commitments as Kangaroo tours and the time I needed off to attend Origin camps. I began to feel stale and after a lot of soul-searching I decided to throw my energies into making the most of the opportunities football was offering. Seven long years on it is even tougher for a player to hold down the two careers because the demands of the modern game are too great. I was a sympathetic observer as Balmain's promising lock,

Displaying my 1986 Rugby League Writers Rookie of the Year Award. Parramatta legend Peter Sterling was named Player of the Year.

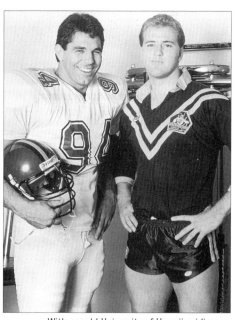

With my old University of Hawaii gridiron team-mate, Colin Scotts

Stammering my way through a 2KY radio interview with David Lord, I suffered terrible shyness when I was first graded.

Sirro as a long-haired junior with stars in his eyes
Sironen Family

Even as a toddler Sirro was blessed with big thighs.
Sironen Family

Garry Jack reminds Wayne Pearce about the three bucks he borrowed from him at training.

'Sirro' on the the boil

Benny Elias remembers he forgot to ring his cousin to say happy birthday.

Few players have worn the green and gold of Australia with more pride than Wayne Pearce.

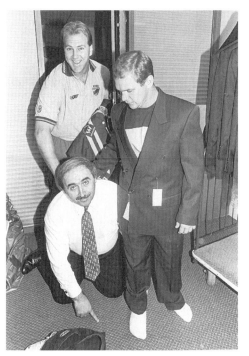

Not a Lowes commercial, Arthur Coorey the official outfitter to the ARL is resigned to chopping up a pair of trousers to fit Allan Langer for a Kangaroo tour.

The original wild child of League, Kerry Hemsley lets his hair down.

Tim Brasher pretending to be Mike Tyson during State of Origin training

Few players had their opponents walk on eggshells like Steve Roach.
Andrew Varley

Bustling Bobby Lindner was another bloke accused of not giving his all in club football.

Its one of my big regrets that my shyness didn't allow me to get to know Wally Lewis on the Kangaroo tour.

Move over Mel Gibson — Sammy Backo on the rampage

Andrew Varley

One of the game's hardest men, Les Davidson

Two old boilers savor a 1996 grand final win —
Des Hasler and Dave Gillespie.

Laurie Daley is one of the game's
most loved characters.

Mark Geyer is one bloke you'd want next to you
in the trenches.

The $700,000 man,
Timmy Brasher

Greg Alexander and I shared the disappointment of missing the 1982 Australian Schoolboys tour.

Action Photographics

Clyde by name, Clydesdale by nature, Brad Clyde

Peter Sterling was good enough to get away with anything . . . even serving a footy on the tennis court.

Mean Gene Miles

Glenn Morrison, tried to shuffle his life around police work and ball work last year. It came as no surprise to me when he decided to chuck the police duties in. The poor kid was playing first grade against such sides as Manly, Canberra and Norths on a measly two hours' sleep, thanks to his shifts! Nevertheless, I think it is a damn pity that the sight of a beefy footballer keeping the streets safe appears destined to be a thing of the past. Apart from developing a countenance of authority and a readiness to follow orders in most footballers, it was also a job that allowed them to learn a lesson or two about life.

THE ROOKIE

CHAPTER 6

My most immediate observation as a first grade rookie wasn't so much of the tough training sessions or intense team meetings but of the baggings that went on in the dressing room. They shocked me most of all because they *really* were something else. The bulk of the comments were downright cutting. The blokes would be picked on for such things as the size of their ears, their choice of clothes, the way they spoke, the way they walked, or even the girl they were seen out with the previous weekend. What amazed me most of all was the fact no-one seemed to take any of it personally . . . there was an unspoken rule that you copped it square on the chin. Well, while I may have been big and ugly enough to look after myself on the footy paddock, I used to hide in the corner of the shed to avoid drawing any attention to myself when things heated up between the boys. Sure, I was the class clown at school, but at Balmain I figured discretion the better part of valour. I was among some real masters of gee-ups and insults! My apprehension stemmed back to my incredible shyness at the time I was promoted to first grade in the third round of the 1986 Winfield Cup premiership. I found it a tough task just to call for the ball during a game, so I'm sure you'd agree it really wasn't in me at that stage of my career to trade insults or wisecracks with the senior blokes. While I could more than match myself against those fellows now, I was smart enough to realise back then that most of them would've had me on toast in a slanging match.

Nevertheless, Kerry 'Buckets' Hemsley—the wild child of the Tigers pack—seemed to take a perverse delight in my discomfort. Kerry is one of those blokes who can smell fear a mile off, and after spending hours mulling over my predicament he dubbed me 'Telecom' because he reckoned I walked about like a bloke carrying telephone books. The insinuation was I strutted around with my chest puffed out and my arms pumped up like one of those Arnold Schwarzenegger wannabes you see hanging about any gymnasium. A few players gave Buckets their thumbs up for his creativity, but I'm grateful 'Telecom' lost out to 'Sirro' as my nickname. Despite Buckets' obvious enjoyment in trying to make me squirm at any possible opportunity, I couldn't help but like him because he was a long-haired prop with real attitude. He'd rumble along to footy games on his '64 Harley Davidson and then play footy as if he was League's answer to Marlon Brando—you know, tough and rebellious. Buckets also loves his beer and if you're crazy enough to want to get on his bad side just buy him a middy, because the chances are he'll let the glass slip through his drinking hand and snarl, 'These hands were made for schooners, pal!'

Nevertheless, Buckets was a true Balmain boy and I've long respected the fact he rejected a lucrative offer to join Illawarra all because he was a dozen games short of playing 100 games for the Tigers. He loved his club and mates too much to leave. 'I was just being polite by listening to them,' he told the boys when news broke of the deal. As a rebel without a cause, however, Kerry had some run-ins with a few of my police colleagues for a variety of reasons that are better left unsaid, and even as a raw rookie cop and footballer I could always tell when Kerry was primed to bellyache about his latest brush with so-called police harassment because he'd get an angry look in his eyes. I'd learned the hard way that that was one conversation *not* to get dragged into, so whenever I noticed that look I'd nip it in the bud by saying, 'Hemmo, I don't want to hear it, mate!'

Kerry wasn't the only one who wanted to lumber me with an unwelcome moniker—Russell Gartner, the former Manly and Aus-tralian centre, liked to call me 'Felix', as in *Felix the Cat*. That was

'Frogs'-eyes' way of letting me know he thought I sometimes played like a pussy and, believe me, it was hard not to bite at that crack, especially when a few other champion Balmain baggers, such as Gary Bridge and Garry Jack, were happy to run with Felix until I proved myself. I followed the unwritten law to cop it sweet until I felt as though I was accepted as a part of the team and was more confident within myself. Then I enjoyed swinging with the best of them. While I may have been the unknown face of the Tigers pack when I was given my first grade spurs in 1986, *Rugby League Week*'s then editor Ian Heads was tipped off about me by Frank Stanton in 1985 when I was playing reserve grade, and he did a full-page colour feature on me. It was a great thrill to appear in the 'Bible', and since I was a kid the RLW was the closest thing to a book that I enjoyed reading. I once owned the entire collection from 1973 to 1983, but my mum made me chuck 'em in the bin when some silverfish got to them—because I treasured them I found throwing them out akin to putting a pet dog to sleep!

While I've never allowed for myself to get too carried away with any publicity, it was difficult to contain my pride when I read a few heavy dudes such as our chief executive Keith Barnes, coach Frank Stanton and even Heads wrap me up. Heads, one of the game's most respected journos, advised his readers to jot my name down in their little black book as a player to watch, while Barnes said he'd be shocked if I failed to do something in football: 'I'll be surprised if he doesn't make it because he's got all that it takes.'

Reading that article was a great incentive for me to work even harder in the gymnasium Rod and I had put together in the family garage. Apart from heaving weights I also ran along the old bush track at the back of the house just like I did when I was a kid with grand dreams of making the big time. And I don't mind admitting that in 1985, I felt as though that childhood fantasy was suddenly well within my reach—and that thought made me the happiest bloke in East Ryde. There was one hairy moment in my season as a Balmain reserve grader, however, and that was the day I suffered a head knock against Illawarra. I can't remember anything of the game, but I'm told when I started to choke on my mouthguard Steelers hooker Michael Bolt was quick to remove it and he then rolled me over on my side and cleared my passageway so I wouldn't choke on my tongue. One very nervous person sitting in the grandstand was my mother and after she learned of Bolt's actions she wrote him a letter of gratitude and sent him something like ten scratch lottery tickets. I'm indebted to what Michael did for me, but I couldn't believe it when I learned what Mum had done. Talk about making a bloke look like a real gig!

At the end of '85 the Rabbitohs offered me a rather tempting deal to play at Redfern. Part of the package included a decent contract for Rod. While I decided to stay put at Balmain, Rod trialled with Souths since the Tigers had a glut of second-rowers, including Paul McCabe, Michael Campbell, David Brooks and Kevin Hardwick. We locked horns against one another in a preseason match in 1986 and I remember it well because the bugger was around my legs *every* time I caught the ball. I'd never before been marked as closely as that and I realised that was Rod's pride on show—he didn't want his little brother to get the better of him. He needn't have felt like that, because as a footballer I'll always remember my big brother as a more than handy player. He was strong, he had a great work ethic and he was a tremendous team man. Nevertheless, because Rod saw his future in the building game he turned his back on grade football to work many long and hard hours alongside Dad. He didn't abandon the game completely, but continued playing A-grade football in the North Sydney juniors, and he won a few premierships with Lane Cove and McMahons Point where he was regarded by his peers as an extremely tough, but fair, competitor.

Apart from enjoying good fortunes on the footy field, things were also very bright on the romance front. I'd bumped into a girl who I went to school with at a local nightclub. Her name was Lee-Anne Webber—it's Lee-Anne Sironen now—and she bowled me over with a force that no tackle has ever managed. Lee-Anne was in the year below me at Malvina High. I could clearly remember her face from the old schoolyard, but we'd never spoken to one another until that night. I suspect the reason we'd never communicated before was because back then she probably considered me as nothing more than a football-playing dork. Nevertheless, I asked her out and we've been together ever since. Actually, I'm glad Lee-Anne has been beside me from the beginning of my first grade career because we've been through all the good and bad times together and I believe that old saying about there being a good woman behind every successful bloke. She's been a definite tower of strength throughout my twelve years in first grade. Strangely, when I think of it, I have no doubt we were destined to meet because we have so many mutual friends.

Hell, I even worked alongside her uncle on a road gang for the Ryde Council when I was waiting to be accepted in the police force. And that was an interesting experience because most of my working day as a 'gangie' was spent killing time by throwing rocks at targets on the other side of the road. While I always thought the plum job on the council was to be the bloke who held the *Stop* and *Go* sign, you can imagine how surprised I was to be promoted to the driver of the big roller that smoothed out the tar—and I was given an extra 40 bucks a week! Don't laugh, because that whacked my weekly pay cheque up to the princely sum of $260—a small fortune for a battling footballer back then.

I was given my call to arms against the mighty Parramatta team in the third round of the 1986 Winfield Cup and that was courtesy of a suspension handed down to Steve 'Blocker' Roach. While I was excited about getting my chance I was also nervous about making my top grade debut because the Eels outfit boasted the likes of Ray Price, Brett Kenny, Peter Sterling and Stan Jurd. I expected it to be a fiery initiation. Those nerves were knocked out of me by the first tackle—not only was it no different from the thousands of others I'd received beforehand, it also helped to settle me down. Nevertheless, I couldn't have picked a tougher outfit to cut my teeth on. Parramatta were the ultimate professionals that sunny afternoon in March. Their pack crushed us with some relentless defence and I still remember the Eels tackling being so intense it not only brought our attack to an embarrassing standstill but it forced us into making basic ball-handling errors. It was a terrible mess. Frank, furious with our collective effort, lived up to his nickname of 'Cranky' during the half-time break. We trailed the Eels 16–0 at half-time and from talking to some people after the game I concluded Frank's anger was justified. The feeling in the grandstand was that we were expected to be blown away in the second half! However, they say through the furnace of adversity are cast men of steel, and I was given my first insight into the legendary Balmain fighting spirit soon after the break when the boys returned to the field breathing fire. Wayne Pearce capitalised on some flashy work by Gary Bridge to score a well-deserved try in the 45th minute, and there was a genuine belief we could spark a fightback and push the Eels all the way. However, the wheels fell off when our dummy-half Benny Elias elected to run the ball on the sixth tackle despite Bridgey's screaming for the ball so he could boot the bloody thing downfield. Unfortunately,

Brett Kenny, Paul Taylor and Neil Hunt combined on the fourth tackle from that turnover to send their rookie centre Brian Jackson over for the match-sealing try.

I was dirty to lose to the Eels on my debut, but I found playing against Price, Kenny and Sterling a tremendous education. Price, the ultimate warrior, made a tremendous impact on me even though it was his final season—he mauled me—and I went home that night thinking the raw-boned, sinewy and *very* angry Ray Price was really something special. He also knew how to sting in defence. He'd landed a few good shots, and you can rest assured I spared an unpleasant thought for him the following morning when the bruises started to surface. The player who taught me what Rugby League was *really* about though, was the tough St George prop Robert Stone, who knew every trick in the book ... like stamping on an opponent's hand as he tried to get up off the ground, and that an elbow has more uses than sinking a few beers.

Straight after the defeat coach Stanton told the press he not only admired the professionalism of the Eels, but he was also amazed by their killer instinct: 'We've given good teams 14 points start and pulled them back. But you can't against Parramatta ... once they have got you on the ropes, you stay on the ropes,' he said.

While I was happy enough with my form, mine was far from the best beginning to a first grade side, and after our third consecutive loss (to Parramatta, Manly and St George) I began to wonder whether I'd jinxed the team. With each defeat the punters were asking what was wrong with Balmain and most of us were stuffed for an answer. Most of us, that is, but coach Stanton. He was adamant when talking to *Rugby League Week* that the Tigers could fight their way out of strife by telling the media:

All is not lost at Leichhardt, and the world is not about to end. I remain convinced we have a football team which can go as far, or further, as we did in '85. The problem is a mental one. In the next two vital weeks we need to regroup, reassess—and recapture the hunger to win games. Each player will need to assess his own individual will to win. All of us need to think about the fact you can play the most attractive football imaginable—but if you don't have steel to back it all up then everything goes to waste.

That was the thing I really liked about Frank—he was a straight-shooter and was never one to shirk the hard issues. While there was no doubt I was enthusiastic and keen about playing, when I reflect on those formative weeks in first grade I recall a big, nervous kid who was too scared to say boo to anyone. I sat in the corner not wanting to be picked on during the bagging sessions, and I also didn't want to tread on my team-mates' toes by calling for the ball or getting in their way during a game. I was terrified of stuffing things up. I think every rookie is confronted by such doubts but it's important they get over them quickly because it's a sad fact of football life that no-one lasts too long if they don't. It took me only a few runs to find my feet in first grade, and once I settled down I enjoyed the experience. I'd pumped up to 105 kilos and I was dubbed the 'Hawaiian Hulk' by some of the media because of my American Football experience. But a few of them could see something more than just a big bloke who loved his footy, and Dom Abouchar from *RLW* said the way I went about playing football was, 'Balmain first, his own body second. Sironen likes to fling his frame hard and fast. Into tackles.' There were a few other stories written about me in my rookie year and in time Mum was cutting all the newspapers to pieces to paste the latest article on me in a scrapbook—but she did it before anyone else had time to read the paper! In one way I wish she hadn't kept some of those early yarns—like the photo a newspaper snapper took of me stripped to my waist and holding a wheelbarrow above my head—because I have a feeling my boys Curtis and Bayley will throw my playing the clown back in my face one day in the future.

Despite such attention there was never any danger of me developing a swelled head, because at a place like Balmain an inflated ego would be way too dangerous ... it would have given the likes of Hemsley, Gartner, Bridge and Roach way too much ammunition to play with. There was also no danger of me trying to make out I was something special to the boys on the road gang either. Some of those guys were real hard nuts and I'm sure they'd have tarred and feathered me if I'd tried to flaunt my sudden success in their face. In saying that, however, I couldn't contain myself when, after just seven games, I saw myself rated as RLW's '86 Kangaroo Candidate No. 24. Accompanying a photo of me running into Parramatta's Michael Moseley was a blurb that said while I was by no means a certainty of boarding the big silver bird to England at season's end, I did have some hope of touring the north of England and the south of France:

> There's no doubting this big fella is a rank outsider for a Kangaroo job, but boy wouldn't he be a handy asset.
>
> Sironen, not yet 21, is one of the biggest players in the Sydney competition. He stands at 193 cm and weighs 105 kg and is turning more and more heads every week with his powerhouse running.
>
> Spotted by gridiron talent scouts while playing in Balmain's juniors, Sironen was whisked off to Hawaii where he tried his hand at the American game. But he returned to his beloved Tigers last year and rocketed up the grades, and he has now established himself as a regular first grader.
>
> Sironen's game is all power, running from deep and hitting the ball at full pace. In defence, the harder he hits, the better he likes it. He's a long-shot, for sure; but not a player who would let any side down.'

The idea of forcing my way onto the tour certainly appealed to me, but I had my reservations as to whether the national selectors would be prepared to gamble on a kid who'd gone from reserves to firsts in the space of a season. And I'll never forget the afternoon I feared I'd blown any slim chance I may have had of snaring a Kangaroo guernsey when referee Greg McCallum sent me from the Wollongong Showground for an alleged head-butt on Trevor Kissell, which was a bloody joke because I was actually trying to protect my crown jewels from being wrenched off! I was confident the judiciary would agree there was no malice in my actions, but a little voice nagged away at the back of my mind: 'What if, Sirro . . . what if?' Fortunately the Tigers toughed it out without me and our twelve-man side beat the odds to scrape home 22–18.

It was a real gutsy effort and I realise the only reason I was spared an ear-bashing from Frank about letting the boys down was because he also considered it a controversial dismissal. Thankfully, I was cleared by the Phillip Street judiciary of any wrongdoing and I threw myself back into the business of playing football. However, it seemed the longer the season went, the more some people were willing to accept me as a genuine candidate for a Kangaroo berth. When I reflect on that time, I reckon it was of an enormous benefit to me that I was surrounded by so many class players because they created plenty of opportunities for me to look good. I also didn't mind mixing it with the opposition's forwards and one of my most satisfying games was playing a strong hand in the Tigers 38–20 win over Souths, the streetfighters who the bookies regarded as strong contenders for the Winfield Cup title.

It was one of those afternoons where we could do no wrong against the likes of Lindsay Johnston, David Boyle, Mario Fenech, Phil Gould and Les Davidson. Our match plan was to rough up the Rabbitohs before they got to us. I took the orders to heart and I not only hit Phil Gould with a good shot under the ribs early in the game but I also managed to crunch their clever lock, Michael Andrews. What was even more satisfying, was managing to suck in a few of their defenders to off-load passes that set up Michael Campbell and the Englishman Garry Schofield for tries. By full-time the critics agreed we'd beaten Souths at their own game—playing rough-house tactics—and each of us felt a great sense of achievement because we'd proven once and for all that not only could we mix it if we needed to, but we could mix it well. Our tough-guy approach stunned Rabbitohs coach George Piggins and he told the journalists: 'Balmain were allowed to play rough and tough; they were allowed to rip in. Next week will be no holds barred like Balmain were— they didn't take any prisoners and as long as they [the refs] allow us to play the same way it will suit us. I'll enjoy it.'

That wasn't our last match-up against the Rabbitohs in '86, and when we played them in the semi-final at the SCG it was another tough game. The scene for a bitter encounter was set just before the kick-off when Benny and Mario sledged one another furiously— it wasn't mere sportsmanship either, it was pure hate, and neither hooker held anything back. As the game progressed it seemed as though the Rabbitoh pre-match tactics were to target Benny and me for some extra attention, and take it from me, we were punished legally—and otherwise. Benny was knocked down three times off the ball while I copped a blatant elbow flush in the face and I also felt a few knees crash into my back as well. The Benny–Mario feud continued well into the game until, in a moment of high drama, referee Kevin Roberts sent Fenech off the field for an alleged eye-gouge in a scrum. Up until Fenech's dismissal the semi was very much in the balance at 8–all, but once the Rabbitohs hooker was dismissed it was pretty much all over. I think the ABC commentator Mike Stephenson summed it up best when he groaned, 'Mario Fenech has spoiled the game for spectators and Souths fans!'

Despite the blow of losing Fenech, the Rabbitohs played with plenty of old-fashioned ticker and it's testimony to their sheer determination that we didn't run away with the game until midway through the second-half. I clearly remember Les Davidson being relentless in defence. I have no doubts anyone was surprised when his name was read out as part of the Kangaroo train-on squad after the match.

But all good things come to an end and we were bundled out of the grand final race the following weekend by a deadly efficient Canterbury outfit, 28–16. We entered the game as wounded Tigers because Wayne Pearce (knee) and Steve Roach (suspension) were sidelined while Benny had a neck problem; David Brooks, Garry Jack and Gary Bridge carried leg injuries and I was suffering from the effects of a virus which left me feeling terribly lethargic. Our collective hardships made our playing the Bulldogs a backs-to-the-wall assignment and a couple of people thought we were on a hiding to nothing against a Canterbury team which wasn't only a lot healthier than us, but one which was also a heck of a lot hungrier.

While I was bitterly disappointed to miss out on playing the eventual premiers, Parramatta, in the grand final during my debut season, the year ended with a series of high notes. I not only won the NSW Rugby League Writers' rookie award but I was awarded the Balmain Players' player trophy and the Tigers rookie of the season. I was honoured to win those awards but the undoubted glittering prize of all was being presented with one of twenty-eight Kangaroo jumpers . . . it was bloody magnificent. You can believe me when I say I jumped for joy on learning of my selection! All I can say on making that tour is, should anyone ever tell you dreams can't come true just laugh at them, because as far as I'm concerned 1986 was a fair dinkum football fairytale.

THE BATTLER

CHAPTER 7

If 1986 was a fairytale season for me then 1987 was a bloody nightmare. Nothing went right. I went from being Cinderella to finishing up as the pumpkin. I'd packed on 8 kilos of fat from eating all the wrong foods in the north of England; I was carting a groin injury about; and my form crashed faster than Wall Street during the Great Depression. People blamed my demise on a supposed Kangaroo curse which is reputed to have affected some players ever since Dally Messenger and the boys sailed away on the first tour in 1908, but I dismissed that as tripe . . . I was simply out of form and I was having trouble finding my way back.

A few of the other tourists, such as Les Davidson, Steve Folkes and Phil Daley, had faltered at the beginning of '87 but they hung in and managed to claw their way back.

However, as I floundered, the pressure began to build up on me to perform and when I hit rock bottom one of the most asked questions bandied about by the press was, 'What's up with Sirro? When's he going to get his act together?' Balmain supporters wanted to see an immediate form turnaround and when that didn't occur a few people bayed for my blood. With each disgruntled cry the pressure mounted on our new coach, Billy Anderson, to drop me to second grade. Bill wasn't keen to axe me, however, perhaps he feared banishing me to reserves would shatter what was left of my flimsy confidence. He might also have believed I was simply a game or two off hitting a purple patch. I've never asked Bill why he stuck with me, but I do know the more he stood by me the greater the pressure I felt to do *something* to repay his faith.

It seemed everyone had the answer to my dilemma. Some people said I had to tap into my confidence and enthusiasm of the previous winter . . . others said I should follow a certain diet . . . others told me to watch videos of myself from the previous year . . . and one upset fan even gave me a copy of a prayer to St Jude, the saint for desperate causes! I was getting desperate, so I spoke to my team-mates and I engaged in numerous deep and meaningful talks with the Tigers coaching staff. In the back of my mind, however, I knew what I really needed, and that was some time away from the paddock to rest and recover from the groin injury I'd brought home from the northern hemisphere. I didn't dare ask Bill for some time off because I didn't want to gain a reputation as a player who wasn't only out of form, but one who thought he was some sort of superstar. In truth, though, I was in agony and I'll never forget the evening I was over at Lee-Anne's grandfather's house and I sneezed. It dead-set felt as though someone had stabbed me with a dagger in the groin and I just about screamed his house down. But that's how it was . . . I needed only to take a sudden knock on the field or sneeze and I'd be crippled. Nevertheless, I had no choice except to play because throughout the season we missed the likes of Steve Roach, Paul Clarke, Kerry Hemsley, Garry Jack and Wayne Pearce to either representative football or injury—it was a case of all hands being needed on deck.

Compounding my form problems was my shiftwork with the police force. I wasn't getting enough rest . . . and I often found myself rushing from the station to training. My whole life had become one major rush and there were days when I would have loved to have just been able to switch off and forget about a few things—like the baggers. The worse thing about the whole experience was feeling as if I'd let my team-mates down . . . I felt like a bit of a log out on the pitch even though I was trying my heart out. (Actually, I think one problem associated with falling into a form slump is apart from the littlest things becoming a major problem you also look for excuses.) One thing about my slump was that my timing was out of kilter and

I tried to explain to journalist David Middleton how that affected me: 'It's a bit like a cricketer, I guess. When his timing is out he really struggles. Look at Greg Chappell a few years ago. He made all those ducks in a row but then his timing suddenly returned and he killed them. Timing in attack is so important. It's just been a fraction out and it has made such a difference.'

Plus I tried to make too many things happen. For instance, against Easts I ignored the fact that it was a wet day and the ball was muddy by trying to throw 'magic' passes which went down like lead balloons. I finished the game looking stupid, and when people asked me why I didn't just lock the ball up and run I couldn't tell them I was desperate, so I'd simply shrug my shoulders and keep walking. Ultimately, the axe fell and I was sent packing to Peter Duffy's reserve grade side. I didn't blame Bill for his decision, he probably should have done it a few weeks earlier, and 'Duff' was great. He told me I'd soon be back on track and he spent a bit of extra time with me to see if he could find the magic formula that would help to make me click. I watched the match videos from '86 and I almost didn't recognise myself—I was running with a high knee action, a loping stride and then there was the big fend . . . but at the time that footage was all but a distant memory.

Thankfully I was offered plenty of support by not only my team-mates but also the supporters, my family and Lee-Anne. I was a bit of a grumpy bastard and while it would have been so easy for her to throw a frying pan at my head Lee-Anne just stood by and did her best to understand. I eventually dug my way out of that awful hole but I think one of the less tasteful legacies from that 'wasteland' period was the fact critics took it upon themselves to watch me like a hawk. It was as if they were waiting for me to slip up on the field again so they could start bagging me. I may have finished '86 by winning some prestigious awards and touring with the Kangaroos, but I completed '87 with a few critics on my back and, even a decade on, I still haven't been able to shake 'em off. They've been like barnacles on a whale!

GRAND FINAL HEARTACHE

CHAPTER 8

When Balmain lined up against Canterbury for the 1988 grand final, *every* player dressed in the black and gold strip was hurting. We were battered and bruised after a horrendous run home which involved sudden-death matches against such tough nuts as Penrith, Brisbane, Manly, Canberra and Cronulla, and the soreness from our schedule ran deep to our bones. There was a positive side to our death-or-glory charge, however, because living on the edge helped forge a genuine belief we had the right stuff to take the Winfield Cup back to our Leagues club. When I gazed at my team-mates just before kick-off—McGuire, Gartner, Pearce, Brooks, Elias, Hanley, Pobjie, Hemsley, Conlon, Jack, Freeman and Neil—I was overcome by a great sense of reassurance because I realised no-one would dare capitulate if Canterbury were to get over the top of us. My mates, I knew, would fight to the death (or in the case of Ellery, until he was knocked senseless). We'd proven in our hard-fought 9–2 preliminary final win over Cronulla the previous week that Balmain could out-tough our opposition.

Indeed, the boys were so convincing against the Sharks that many of the hard-nosed critics who'd been sweating on the Tigers' bubble to burst were forced to concede we had plenty to offer.

Actually, I remember the battle with the Sharks as a cur of a game because Cronulla not only won the scrums 13–10, but they also spent the first forty minutes camped deep in our territory, harassing us with their accurate kicking game. While they had us on the backfoot we did manage to hit back, and it was of great personal satisfaction that I made a barging run up the guts in the 71st minute and found livewire Mick Neil in support. I fed him the ball and the sight of our $5000-a-match English import Ellery Hanley storming onto Meggsy's pass to cross for the only try of the match was one to savour. The four-pointer was a worthy reward for Ellery because he'd been so frustrated by Cronulla's stifling defence he resorted to running from dummy-half with prop-like chargers in an attempt to break the Sharks line.

While we measured that victory in terms of guts and determination, some critics, such as the great Wally Lewis, took special note of the penalty count which finished 9–7 in our favour. The King reckoned referee Michael Stone had been intimidated into 'looking after' us in the wake of the spray Wazza gave Greg McCallum after our controversial loss to Manly in the 20th round of the premiership. It was a fiery affair with the most controversial moment being the indiscretion committed by Steve Roach in the first half after Gary Freeman had scored an apparently fair try for the Tigers. After consulting his touch judge, McCallum ruled a not try and sinbinned Blocker for punching Phil Daley and he awarded a penalty. Ryan went berserk in his post-match press conference and the NSWRL responded by slapping a $3000 fine on him. However, the likes of Lewis believed that the fine was the best investment Balmain made in '88. He said that because the whistleblowers were terrified of feeling the wrath of Wazza they had taken to treating us with kid gloves. Naturally, that was utter rubbish, but the Queensland legend added fuel to the fire by saying to the press, 'Cronulla were unlucky not to get a penalty when the score was 3–2 against. I reckon everything has gone Balmain's way since their coach abused the referee after their last loss five weeks ago.'

When Mick Stone was appointed to referee the grand final, former Parramatta great Ray Price wrote in his *Rugby League Week* column that we'd mastered the best way to work around Stone's style: 'They creep up inside the five metres and get away with it, their second marker jumps the gun yet they were penalised only once against the Sharks,' he said. 'And they are experts at slowing down the play the ball.'

Once we secured our grand final berth it didn't take too long for the mind games to start. The Bulldogs' thirty-year-old coach Phil Gould fired the first salvo by declaring our man, Wazza, couldn't handle pressure. While we dismissed the allegation as ludicrous it surprised many people because Gould was a Ryan protege—firstly as a player with Newtown's 1981 grand final side, and then as the 1987 reserve grade coach at Canterbury! Yet, the apprentice held nothing back when he told the *Sydney Morning Herald* of his master: 'Ryan has had an enormous impact on the game of Rugby League because of the changes he has initiated. But he has a weakness we have seen twice in the past two years. He cannot handle pressure. When he senses the tide of events turning against him he has all the excuses ready . . . '

As you'd expect, Wazza didn't need much prompting to return serve and he advised Gould to run a thumb over the Warren Ryan record. Ryan's coaching record was one most coaches would kill for, and he stressed that very point in the media by scowling, 'Look at my record. Five grand finals in the '80s and if you include Wests under-23s, it is six grand finals with four clubs. Over a nine-year period—I didn't coach in '83—teams I've coached have made it to the grand final six times.'

While Warren didn't give us any indication as to how he *really* felt about Gould's jibe, I'm sure it cut him to the bone. Wok left the Bulldogs at the end of the previous season on bad terms after a falling out with the club's chief executive Peter 'Bullfrog' Moore and a favourite son of the premiership's self-described 'Family Club', Steve Mortimer. And while his name may have been spelt M.U.D. at Belmore, I'm certain Gus Gould was the last bloke Ryan would have expected to be bagged by. However, rather than sounding about it—apart from his 'look at my record' response—I think Gould's comments made the grand final that even bit more personal. We were given an insight into the depth of feeling Ryan held against Canterbury in the lead-up to our 10th round encounter with them when he boomed, 'I don't care if you don't win another game this season . . . beat them . . . beat these bastards!' So we went out and thumped 'em 19–8, and Warren loved it. He lorded it over the Bulldogs by gloating to the press, 'Canterbury looked more as if they were coached by Bullfrog!' Who knows, perhaps that crack was a major reason behind Gus's 'choking' tag . . .

But that round 10 win was considered ancient history as we prepared for the grand final. The Bulldogs had emerged as the premiership frontrunner and few critics tipped us to upset them. We were the sentimental favourites, however, and it seemed as though battlers from all over the place wanted to throw their support behind us. Indeed, I found it a great struggle not to get caught up in the hype that engulfed the Balmain district. It seemed as though everyone was willing us to win, and some people would go to any extreme to find an angle they believed could help us clear our final hurdle. For instance, one supporter contacted the press to tell of the uncanny similarities between us and the last Balmain side to do a grand final victory lap, the legends of '69. The fan noted that under Ryan and Leo Nosworthy, Balmain made it to the grand final during their first year at the helm; both teams boasted high-profile Poms—Hanley and Dave Bolton; wingers (Ross Conlon and Len Killeen) were the goal kickers; and both Balmain sides went into battle without their strike forward—Steve Roach and Artie Beetson— through suspension.

Other journalists tried to capture the spirit of Tiger-town by interviewing Balmain's most famous resident, Olympic great Dawn Fraser, about our chances and by talking to other locals such as some girl who worked in a Balmain bakery; a flamboyant hairdresser who once cut Kevin Hardwick's wife's hair; some firemen and an old coot who played one game for the Tigers in 1929!

It was madness, and as the big game drew closer it became a major logistic problem just to fit our training sessions around the demands for us to front at store appearances, schools, luncheons and a never-ending stream of media commitments. While we could understand everyone wanting their little part of the team, it was an exhausting schedule and our one saving grace was the fact coach Ryan had been there and done it before. Wazza had the perfect formula to help us forget the ballyhoo—he trained us hard. Bloody hard. The crafty old bugger had calculated if a team received an even share of possession it would have the ball for 17 sets of six tackles and because that equated to just over 100 play-the-balls we were drilled to go through 17 sets of six without dropping the ball . . . it was good stuff, and it reinforced our belief that when it came to grand final football, few could match Warren Ryan for knowledge.

The biggest single blow to our grand final preparation was the four match suspension handed down to big Blocker Roach after he collided with Penrith's Chris 'Louie' Mortimer in our play-off match. I agreed wholeheartedly with Steve when he claimed the tackle was an accident because in the instant he committed himself to help Junior chop Mortimer down, Louie fell and collided with the Balmain enforcer. Mortimer was knocked unconscious, but because no action was taken against the tackle on the field, Blocker has long maintained dirty politics was behind his suspension—who knows? Perhaps he is right. I'm certain no-one at Phillip Street could have imagined how Balmain would strike back, however, because it was done with all the intrigue of a James Bond 007 movie. Barnesy enlisted the aid of the top English club Warrington to help the big bloke fulfil his suspension by sitting on the sideline for one of their games and he'd then return Down Under to take his place in the Balmain pack. It was a perfect plan. Having already missed three of our sudden-death games the Warrington match would have made him eligible to play in the grand final. And there was nothing the League could do about it since Mario Fenech, another hothead, had sat out his Sydney suspension while playing for Bradford Northern in 1986 and that manoeuvre went unchallenged by Phillip Street.

Anyway, Blocker loved the idea. Apart from ensuring him a run in the grand final, it also gave him the chance to get the better of his 'enemies' on the judiciary. Once the media got wind of the ruse, however, Phillip Street went ballistic. They pressured Balmain to scrap the idea, and much to Steve's dismay, our hierarchy caved in. While I knew we'd miss him badly, Ray Price suggested the Tigers might be better off not having Roachy out on the SFS when he said, 'This showdown is going to be won or lost on mistakes, on who finishes with thirteen players on the field, and who best "interprets" referee Mick Stone. And Roach would be likely to give away some silly penalties and get trapped in the nonsense, and that could be fatal . . . '

Despite losing Blocker, we thrived on the underdog status—it was as if we were against the world,—and one bloke who really lapped up that feeling was our skipper, Junior. Pearcey told the press, 'We've been rated underdogs and that is a big motivation to do well. The crowd support has been great, a lot of people are hoping we'll win . . . I think Balmain are a popular team around town.'

A few of us, however, had some demons to wrestle. For instance, Benny fielded calls on three consecutive nights from some shady character who told him it would be worth his while to 'throw' the game. The calls shook him up, but when Ben spoke to Keith Barnes about them it was decided to say nothing to the press because Barnesy could see nothing to be gained by highlighting the matter. There were other dramas, such as my second-row buddy David Brooks treading on a nail while working on a building site. Brooksy did it tough in the build-up to the grand final with a dirty big hole in the sole of his foot . . . and then there was me. I was contending with a calf muscle injury I suffered at training. It was only a run-of-the-mill thing, but it was amazing how the pressures of grand final week compounded the problem.

As I've already said, everyone seemed to be tipping Canterbury. Former Australian Test coach Terry Fearnley and his successor Don Furner both predicted a Bulldog victory, with Furner maintaining the Bulldogs thrived on pressure. Fearnley dismissed us on the basis that we'd not only miss our upfront enforcer, but that the experience of Peter Tunks, Paul Dunn, Steve Folkes, Dave Gillespie and Paul Langmack give Canterbury the edge. He believed Balmain's big worry would be, having finally reached the grand final, we'd have to pick ourselves up one more time after weeks of playing sudden death.

The more we were expected by such experts to lose, the more it seemed that Warren enjoyed himself. He realised we were on a roll and, as for Canterbury, he knew intimately each of their player's strengths and weaknesses. He figured we had the aces up our sleeves, but he warned us not to give the Bulldog ball-runners like Langmack and Lamb any room to move or they'd carve us up.

If anything bothered me in the lead-up to the game it was our lack of grand final experience. As Fearnley suggested, you only needed to glance at the Bulldogs' playing record to realise they were rich in experience. They had guys such as Steve Folkes, who'd played in five, Peter Tunks and Andrew Farrar, who'd been in three, Michael Hagan and Terry Lamb, who'd been there twice. Our only veteran was Russell 'Frogs'-eyes' Gartner, who'd played in two for Manly in the late 1970s—a lifetime ago in Rugby League terms. That was only a passing concern, however, because there was a real positive vibe at Balmain, and people such as the victorious 1969 coach Leo Nosworthy were telling the press we rated very highly compared to any of the Tigers' great sides because, 'We had some marvellous players in my time as well. Like this year, we got the wind at our backs at the end of the year and couldn't be held back.'

We were shielded from many unwanted distractions, but I reckon the biggest mistake the club made was to whack on a luncheon at the Leagues club the afternoon *before* the title-decider. As far as blunders go, I think that luncheon must rank with Parramatta's infamous ticker-tape parade a few days *before* they played (and lost) the 1976 grand final. You see, when we entered the auditorium it was akin to a victory celebration. People were chanting 'Tigers . . . Tigers', the hierarchy auctioned off our jumpers and ran other raffles and poured copious amounts of expensive champagne into the glasses of the seemingly insatiable horde. It was everything we had tried to avoid, and to this day I'm certain I saw Warren roll his eyes in disbelief at the scene before him.

As part of the festivities to help celebrate the first grand final at the $65 million Sydney Football Stadium, the ARL released 51 000 red and white balloons into the blue Sydney sky. To this day I'm still at a loss as to know what they signified, but I do remember thinking my standing in the middle of the stadium before 40 000 spectators and a worldwide television audience estimated to be in their millions was a definite career highlight.

There is nothing quite like the feeling of playing in a grand final. While I'll always maintain that representing Australia is the greatest honour any player can attain, simply qualifying for the grand final is a brilliant team achievement. It is the end result of marrying some great football with a tremendous team spirit. And on that day it felt as though everything was on the line. As the crowd sang the national anthem I thought about the many hurdles we'd overcome just to make it to the grand final—surviving weeks on end of sudden-death football, fighting on without Blocker and thumbing our noses at the critics who thought we weren't tough enough to survive the grind . . .

It took only two minutes for both teams to try and exert their authority over the other—a wild brawl broke out and it was on for young and old. It wasn't anything spiteful, just a few boofy blokes letting off some pent-up steam. If I remember correctly I think Benny was at the centre of it, making a crack about Peter Tunks's hair—or rather, the lack of it. It was just part of the traditional softening-up period, and when referee Mick Stone finally restored order he advised Steve Folkes, Terry Lamb, Gary Freeman and Kerry Hemsely to calm down. However, in the fifth minute of play Tunksy was sinbinned for flattening Benny in an illegal tackle . . . I guess he didn't appreciate Benny's sledge about his balding head. The loss of their captain made the Bulldogs step up a gear, and it was almost impossible for us to move. The pressure they exerted was amazing. It could have been interpreted as a backhanded tribute to the bloke who'd helped construct their defensive pattern for them in the first place, Warren Ryan.

We had to wait until the 20th minute to hit the lead, and it came courtesy of a Benny Elias special. The little bloke scored a try off his own bomb and it was brilliant to see the crowd turn into an ocean of black and gold flags and streamers. But seven lousy minutes later, a tackle changed the entire course of the game . . . the tackle in which Andrew Farrar and Terry Lamb combined to crunch Ellery Hanley in what appeared to be a run-of-the-mill hit. Poor Pearl had no idea of where he was . . . but when he was carted off the paddock to clear his head we expected him to make a quick return because he has long been a player blessed with the ability to soak up an enormous amount of punishment. But not this time. It was a cruel blow for the Great Britain Test skipper because that hit denied him any chance of creating history by playing in a victorious Wembley side and a NSWRL premiership-winning team in the same year.

I've heard some people criticise Hanley for not coming out to play in the second half but the truth is, he was stuffed. Warren sent him back on the field two minutes before half-time, but it was useless—Ellery was off with the pixies. By the time Pearl returned the Bulldogs had inflicted plenty of damage on us by scoring a try soon after he was assisted from the fray. The few moments leading up to that try will plague the Tigers of '88 for the rest of their lives, a point *Rugby League Week*'s Neil Cadigan made clear when he wrote, 'There has never been such an obvious turning point or costly sequence of missed tackles in recent grand finals than the few seconds which Balmain will rue for the next twelve months before Hagan scored.'

It was nightmare material. Not long after Scott Gale replaced Ellery, Canterbury's big Andrew Farrar stepped inside during a Bulldog raid and pushed Scotty off before off-loading the ball to his winger Glen Nissen, a genuine speedster. I did my best to come across in cover, but Nissen was too quick and he ran around me before stepping past Gary Freeman . . . and as I saw Mick Hagan catch the ball and sprint the last 25 metres to score, a feeling of dread overwhelmed me. Canterbury led 12–6 at half-time, and while it was an attainable scoreline they definitely had their tails up.

We believed we could strike back, but without Hanley we lacked the pizzazz that had made us such a force to be reckoned with in our great run home. I later learned that, on the other side of the tunnel, the Canterbury dressing room was overflowing with confidence. Phil Gould told the *Daily Telegraph*'s Ray Chesterton he impressed upon his troops the belief Canterbury were only forty minutes away from a historic victory. 'We talked about being champions,' he said. 'We talked about the victory lap, and we talked about what was needed to get there. We decided we had to play them in the middle and it had to be the forwards that led the way . . . '

Well, their forwards followed his instructions all right because they led the way. Our tough run into the grand final began to show in the middle of the second half when our tiredness and soreness caught up with us. It was hard to pick ourselves up after making a tackle and running the ball became a real chore. It felt as though we were moving in slow motion. But despite the pain, we vowed not to allow the game to degenerate into a landslide victory for the Bulldogs once they started to get a roll on. Junior was a constant inspiration and seeing him take the fight to Canterbury when our backs were to the wall spurred me on. In fact, it is still a matter of some personal satisfaction that I barrelled the eventual man of the match, Paul Dunn, with two big hits in the second half. Unfortunately, it was to no avail. The Bulldogs effectively wrapped up the grand final at 4.18 pm when David Gillespie crashed over the line for a try . . .

It's hard to explain what it feels like to lose a grand final. It is a hollow feeling, and there's no escaping the press photographers and television cameramen determined to capture the sorry portrait of defeat. Yeah, the sting of a grand final defeat is so terrible it reduces you to tears and even a feeling of terrible shame. And as much as I was disappointed by the loss, Wayne was beyond consoling . . . it took him a while to snap out of feeling like a failure.

For their part Canterbury were gracious winners. To a man they came over and shook our hands and thanked us for what they described as a good battle. Most of the post-match formalities are a blur to me now, but I do remember swapping my jumper with Steve Folkes and wishing the presentations would be over and done with so we could lock ourselves in the dressing room and be alone with our thoughts for a while.

Warren Ryan was in some of the Canterbury boys' thoughts as they whooped up their 24–12 win. Paul Langmack and Paul Dunn attributed the Ryan touch to the Bulldogs' success. 'In a way he has paid for being such a good coach,' said Langmack. 'Warren laid the foundations and Phil put the icing on the cake!' And Dunn, the Churchill Medal winner, revealed he psyched himself up for the match of his life by reading handwritten motivational messages Wazza had penned for him the year before in a bid to help lift him out of a form rut. 'I don't know if Warren would like to hear it right now, but they acted as a grand final spur,' Dunn said. 'He gave it to me last year when I was playing like an old woman. I came back from the Kangaroo tour a bit big-headed, I'll admit, and my form went down. Warren helped me get my mind back on the job and at the end of the season I regained my confidence and my form.'

Well, that was the final insult, and we Balmain boys drowned our sorrows at the numerous watering holes around our district. The strange thing was that no matter how much grog we consumed it didn't help exorcise the terrible feeling that accompanied our losing the big one. While I sought solace in the fact that we did well to merely qualify for the grand final, it still hurts even after all these years to reflect on that game.

And do you know what hurts even more than losing the 1988 grand final? It's the memory of our shot at the 1989 title . . .

MORE TEARS AND HEARTACHE

CHAPTER 9

M oments before we ran out for our date with destiny—an all-or-nothing grand final against Canberra—Warren Ryan gathered us in a circle and demanded our undivided attention. With all the dramatics of a Shakespearian actor, Wazza threw his silver runners-up medal from the previous year's grand final down on a bench and then produced one of the gold medals he'd won with Canterbury. He held it up to the light and asked just one question: 'Well, what is it going to be this time—gold or silver?'

If ever a team entered a grand final as raging hot favourites, then it was the Balmain Tigers of 1989. Not only had we proven our mettle throughout the season but we were a much better side for playing in the previous year's grand final. Our forward pack ranked as easily the best in the premiership and during the run home into the semi-finals there was no stopping us. We went into overdrive and there was a real purpose in our football, so much so that I ran out onto the Sydney Football Stadium feeling like a bloke who knew he'd bought the winning lottery ticket. But 100 minutes later my euphoria was crushed.

When the full-time siren sounded after extra time, it was time for the boys in black and gold to again ponder a dream that went horribly wrong. And it doesn't come as all that much consolation that critics rate the grand final of '89 as perhaps the best in the history of the game. I personally believe we cost ourselves the premiership by missing too many vital tackles and making terrible mistakes. If you read the history books, however, you'd swear the result hinged on two things—Warren Ryan replacing Blocker and me in the dying stages of the game (and in the dark old days before unlimited interchange), and the very questionable penalty awarded against us when Bill Harrigan penalised Bruce McGuire for 'shepherding' Canberra's hooker Steve Walters as he ran back onside. They were cruel blows, but unlike most people I find it very hard to hold anything against Warren for resting me and Blocker late in the day. We were big blokes back then—we're even bigger now—and we were both tiring as the game, played at breakneck pace, started to reach its dying stages. Wazza figured it would be best to rest us, and nine times out of ten it would have been the right option. As Ryan said after the loss when he replaced Blocker with Kevin Hardwick, and then me with Mick Pobjie, we were in front 14–8 and I suppose he figured we had the premiership in the bag.

However, if *that* was the case I reckon it was one of the few times Warren had forgotten how unpredictable the game of Rugby League can be. I've read his explanation for the controversial changes and I find it hard to crucify him, because as he told *Rugby League Week*: 'With time running out, and the team in front, it is logical to replace tiring big men with players who will tackle. At that stage of the game we didn't need to score any more points, just keep them from scoring. When the bigger blokes are fatigued they cannot recover and get back into the defensive line quickly enough. And Canberra had fortified their team with attacking players.'

Instead, Wazza preferred to point the finger of blame at not only the lopsided 8–2 penalty count but Harrigan's decision to penalise McGuire for 'obstruction' as he ran behind a defending player (Walters) trying to get back onside. In the ensuing set of tackles from that penalty, Raiders fullback Gary Belcher managed to cross our line. Wazza spat venom when he wrote:

> I will debate until the day I die that the penalty against McGuire was wrong. It should have been against Canberra. McGuire tapped the ball forward legally in the play-the-ball because there was no-one in front of him while returning from an offside position, and

Bruce ran into the back of him—yet the penalty went the other way.

The referee, according to the players, reckoned McGuire was using Walters as an obstruction. For the life of me I can't see how you can use an opposition player for obstruction. He's supposed to tackle you. Now, if he's not legally in a position to tackle you he should be penalised for impeding the progress of a player in possession with the ball.

I couldn't argue with his reasoning on either the Walters incident or replacing Blocker, and I under the circumstances Ryan spelled out. I was taken off the paddock just before Canberra winger John Ferguson scored in the 78th minute to give his skipper Mal Meninga a shot at goal, which took the match into extra time. I'll never forget how my heart sank as big Mal booted the two points and then, twenty painful minutes later, Blocker and I were sitting next to each other in the grandstand, shattered witnesses to what may have been a great Canberra victory but was, God knows, a swift kick in the guts to Balmain.

Unlike a few of my old team-mates, I don't hold Warren personally accountable for the loss. Our benched second-rower David Brooks and Blocker, however, both pointed at Ryan for what they called a massive 'blunder'. Brooks, who seemed to fall out of favour with Wazza just before the finals series, went to town straight after the defeat by telling *Rugby League Week*'s David Middleton, 'At a time when we needed to call on all our experience, all our experience was sitting on the bench,' he fumed. 'Sirro and Roach are our two most experienced players, and "Frog's eyes" [Russell Gartner] and myself were left sitting there. What were we supposed to do—play with ourselves?'

Blocker gave a public insight into his frustrations of that day a few years later in his book, *Doing My Block*, when he wrote: 'I was filthy on everyone when I was replaced. I just couldn't think straight. The only thing going through my head was, "Why did he do it?" I'm still asking myself the same question years later. I've never bothered to ask Ryan why he bothered to make that last decision and he's never bothered to offer me an explanation. Offering explanations is not one of his long suits.'

It's ironic how some things written in the press can rebound on a player, because a few days before the grand final Blocker wrote in his magazine column that he had no problem with being replaced late in a game . . . the big bloke saw it as a bit of a pat on the head when he wrote: 'Some people have said I looked upset at being replaced before the end of my last two games but nothing could be further from the truth . . . I take it as a compliment, actually. If we were getting beaten I'm sure Warren wouldn't take me off. Sure, it would be nice to finish but if it meant winning I don't care what he does.'

As I've already said, I'm certain Warren thought he was doing the right thing when he hooked Blocker and then me. I'm sure if he had access to a crystal ball and could see the consequences of that decision then he'd never have made the changes. Instead, *we* players should shoulder the blame. *We* made way too many errors and by doing so *we*, not Ryan, kept Canberra in the hunt long after they should have been shut out. But, what do we do about that now? The memory of that defeat is one of the real sore points of my career, it still hurts, but blaming Warren Ryan isn't going to change the outcome. I mean, I conceded a penalty when I dived on a loose ball from an offside position and gave Meninga a 'gift' two points to put the Raiders on the board; Blocker was penalised for an indescretion in a tackle; and there were a few of us who missed important tackles. But we have no choice but to learn to live with them . . . and as a player who benefited so much from Ryan's guidance, I hope the 'master' coach has as well.

I haven't ever watched a video of that grand final . . . I can't bring myself to do that because I know I'll end up going through a whole packet of tissues before the game finishes with the Raiders hugging their replacement forward Steve Jackson after he scored his match-sealing try in the 97th minute. And I know I'll scream the house down at the image of our close calls, like Meninga's desperate ankle tap which brought Micky Neil down 5 metres near Canberra's line . . . *Christ*, I thought Meggsy was going to do it . . . I really thought he was going to score. Then, a minute later with men to spare out wide, poor old Junior knocked the ball on, and that was too bloody cruel for words. For Junior, the son of the Leichhardt Oval's former caretaker, the guy who sold hotdogs at Leichhardt Oval on matchday during his childhood and the bloke who inspired us throughout the season, it would have been a great moment to savour—to score in a grand final—but as was to be the order of that day for Balmain it wasn't to be. Benny's field goal which hit the crossbar was another close call, and how about when Brasher retrieved a Gary Freeman chip kick? Until Belcher came on the scene and cleaned him up with a tremendous tackle, I thought he was in. I'm told all our lives are full of missed chances and opportunities lost, but I think on that Sunday afternoon in late September '89 we Balmain boys used up all our lifetime's worth of lost shots.

I do think about the lead-up to that match from time-to-time, however, because by doing so I recall what was probably my best-ever year of club football. We lifted ourselves above the terrible despair of losing the '88 grand final to Canterbury to achieve so much. We quickly found our rhythm and there appeared to be very few teams that could match us for toughness and resolve—especially when we were able to finally field our full strength side from the nineteenth round and onwards—we didn't lose a game. With four rounds remaining there were eight teams who, statistically speaking, could make the final five: Souths on 30, Penrith 26, Cronulla 24, us on 22, defending premiers Canterbury on 21 and Brisbane, Parramatta and Canberra were all locked on 20.

We watched as team after team fell by the wayside and had it not been for a 10–all draw with Manly in the second-last round, we could easily have been one of those sides. We just went through the motions against the Sea Eagles and worse still, when things started to go wrong, the boys started arguing among themselves . . . it was the worst possible scenario. We were lucky not to lose and as Manly's Mal Cochrane's last-minute conversion swung wide, we all felt as if the Tigers had been granted an extra life and we vowed to make the most of it. We went out the following weekend and smashed Penrith 33–6 in a fiery encounter at Leichhardt. When we played Penrith the following week in the knockout semi-final, we bundled them out of the grand final race 24–12. In the game the Panthers coach Ron Willey was criticised for replacing veteran Chris Mortimer with the fresh-faced rookie Brad Fittler just thirty minutes before kick-off. We made the most of Mortimer's absence to take an eight-point lead—it was one the Panthers couldn't catch and it set the standard for our other games in the finals.

Once it became known we'd be playing Canberra in the decider we became the punter's friend, and celebrities such as rock singer Jimmy Barnes and television star Simone Buchanan echoed what had fast become the street corner tip, Balmain to win. I don't think our starting as favourites lulled *most* of us into a false sense of security—the pain of the previous year's defeat was far too strong for that. But Benny dropped his guard when he was asked by the press why we were so cocky and he answered, 'Because no side can beat us.' Unfortunately, those words came back to haunt him. Ben's slip-up aside, we weren't allowed to get carried away. As Canberra was beating Souths 32–16 to force their way into the grand final, we were being put through our paces in a torturous two-hour session by our conditioner Les Hobbs.

It was a real dog of a session. We dressed in our playing strip and spent two hours being 'bashed up'. We ran for two hours, we did plenty of tackling practice and then we were forced to do heaps of stomach exercises. I hate stomach exercises, they hurt at the best of times, but there was method to Hobbsy's madness—he wanted to vary our training sessions to keep us on our toes. Although it seemed we had the bulk of the public support, some critics pinpointed our centre partnership of schoolboy Timmy Brasher and Englishman Andy Currier as weak links in our outfit. They said Timmy was too young and inexperienced to mark the awesome Australian Test centre Mal Meninga, and that Andy Currier lacked the defensive crunch to bother Mal and his centre partner, Laurie Daley, who was rated as one of the game's rising stars. Their lack of confidence didn't phase us, least of all 'Brash' Brasher, who had more confidence than Muhammad Ali. As for Currier, there were some people who rated him a much better signing for us than the charismatic Ellery Hanley who had called Balmain home throughout the previous season. Amazingly, Currier was signed sight unseen because the club's hierarchy was desperate to recruit a class centre after we missed out on re-signing Hanley and Garry Schofield.

Keith Barnes offered Currier a contract after Blocker spoke of him in glowing terms. Apart from making an impression on Roachy (while he was in England with Warrington) with his skill and speed, Currier made a mighty impact on Block when he stood up to one of the real tough guys, Les Davidson, in a heated Warrington–Widnes match. And he not only showed ticker with the Tigers but he became something of a pointscoring machine. After missing the opening nine rounds of the premiership, he still managed to kick 120 points before the semi-finals at an average of 11 points a game.

One of Currier's trademarks was to take what seemed to be an eternity before taking his shot at goal—and he made no apologies for chewing up a few more seconds than the average kicker by saying, 'Yeah, I take my time. The time to black out everything else. The crowd noise and all of that. To get my concentration right I just look at the black strip between the posts, hold it in my mind and imagine the ball going through.' I brushed the criticism about our Englishman off as 'one of those' things, but Blocker went to the press with a word of warning for the Canberra thoroughbreds. He seethed: 'All this talk about Currier not being able to handle Meninga and Daley is rubbish. The way I look at it they have got to catch Currier and Tim Brasher. They have to worry about how good they are on their own feet.'

The club's hierarchy tried to make the week leading into the grand final as relaxed as it possibly could, but poor old Jimmy Jack felt the full wrath of the law when he fronted to training forty-five minutes late and not only missed a scheduled media free-for-all but also a few minutes of our team talk. Even though Jimmy had been among our most consistent players all year, the club had to maintain standards and they fined our fullback $500. The look on Garry's face when he heard he had to dip into his pocket—and big time— was one of absolute pain. Jimmy is renowned for being careful with his cash and I'm sure for him that fine was akin to having an organ forcibly removed.

As the *Sun Herald*'s Alan Clarkson reported on the morning of the match, Garry had the chance to recoup that cash—and more— by helping to win the grand final, because the winner had the chance to pocket $600 000, which up until then represented the biggest payout in the history of Rugby League in Australia. Clarkson pointed out $350 000 of that figure would come out of the winning Australian team's share of the gate for the World Club championship against English team Widnes at Old Trafford. The money sounded great, but as Keith Barnes said, Balmain was playing for more than mere cash: 'I don't care about money, that will be the icing on the cake,' he said. 'We want the Winfield Cup . . . it's as simple as that.'

Mine probably wasn't the best preparation for a grand final. I was working the graveyard shift at the police station and I wasn't sleeping too well. Working wasn't too bad, it took my mind off the battle ahead, but trying to catch some sleep during daylight hours was a bloody nightmare. The more I tried to sleep, the harder it became to switch off and I thought a lot about our opposition from the nation's capital. Everyone said Balmain would win it through the forwards but instead of counting sheep to try and get to sleep, I imagined the Raiders pack. The images of Glenn Lazarus, Steve Walters, Brent Todd, Dean Lance, Gary Coyne and Brad Clyde chilled me to the bone.

They may have been under-rated but I had a lot of time for their pack. Actually, I had a lot of respect for the Raiders. They were a much better team than their fourth place on the ladder suggested. They lost three games while all their stars were away on tour with the Australian side, plus their style of football was flash Harry stuff—they could throw a ball around. Thankfully, as the big game drew closer, a colleague helped put an end to the hours of lying in bed with a cold sweat when he volunteered to swap shifts with me to help me prepare for the big one. That was one offer I didn't need to think twice about!

The first half of the grand final flew in the face of the experts' predictions. They tipped the Tigers would do all the pressing while Canberra was the team to jag a try out of nothing . . . when the crunch came, we jagged a few first-half tries against the run of play and they did plenty of pressing. While we hadn't been the better team, it seemed with our 12–2 lead at the break that we were a mere forty minutes away from a victory lap. Sadly, it wasn't to be. With ninety lousy seconds left on the clock Raiders five-eighth Chris O'Sullivan launched a high bomb towards our posts and I still have no idea of how he managed it, but Laurie Daley got a hand to the loose ball and somehow flicked it out to Canberra's evergreen winger John 'Chicka' Ferguson who breezed past the tackles of Benny Elias, Mick Neil and James Grant to take the Raiders within two points of our 'winning' scoreline. It was a marvellous fairytale finish for Ferguson, who'd played in the 1981 grand final for the Warren Ryan-coached Newtown Jets. When Mal Meninga booted his conversion I had the same feeling of dread I felt twelve months earlier when Glen Nissen scored a try for Canterbury in that grand final. Only this time there was nothing I could do to try to help change the course of the game . . . I was on the bench with Blocker. As the Raiders hit their straps in extra time I felt as helpless as a bloke in a life raft adrift on the open sea. I'd been happy with my own effort because I felt I'd hit their line with some good runs, and Blocker, Junior, Bruce McGuire and Steve Edmed also made some good inroads. It was a tough game and for Canberra their stand-out player was young lock Bradley Clyde, who rounded off an outstanding season by winning the Clive Churchill medal. The award came on top of his breaking into the Australian and NSW team in his first full season of grade football. He'd made the whole football world sit up and take notice of his coming of age. I still can't believe it when I think this was the same kid who wondered whether he was tough enough to survive in first grade after he was mauled by the Tigers back in 1988. He survived all right, and he threw it all back in our faces in the grand final.

Apart from the bitter taste of defeat, two of my most poignant memories of the grand final are of Kerry Hemsley, with a bottle of Jack Daniels in hand, abusing a Canberra supporter who was waving his flag in Bucket's face just before full-time and of Blocker giving Bill Harrigan a mouthful of abuse as the referee left the field. He was smarting over a few things, such as being replaced and Harrigan's lopsided 8–2 penalty count, and had it not been for Junior's timely intervention it could have developed into a very ugly incident. To Harrigan's credit he refused to take any action when quizzed by the referee's coordinator and he said Blocker had only acted in the emotion of the moment. It was a decent gesture . . . I think it was pretty noble of Harrigan to realise that was Steve's way of coping with a heartbreaking loss.

Dealing with the defeat was something we all had to do. Initially we sought solace by getting smashed with whatever grog we could get our hands on, but that terrible, empty feeling remained long after the hangover disappeared. You see, unlike the loss of the '88 grand final where I found comfort in the thought that we'd defied the odds just to make it through to the grand final after finishing fifth, it was too bloody tough to bite the bullet in '89 . . . It took me a few days to look at myself in the mirror because I thought we were going to do it. God, I'd have bet my life on it.

SINGIN' THE BLUES

CHAPTER 10

I've never known any form of football that has been played with the same level of competitiveness, or brutality, as the State of Origin. Rugby League is a real man's sport, and as a result, it is rich with accounts of bravery, such as the time when the 'Little Master', Clive Churchill, kicked a vitally important goal for Souths in the '50s with his broken arm hanging limply by his side. There are graphic photos of a broken-jawed Johnny Sattler spearheading the Rabbitohs to the 1970 premiership title, and the inspirational Rorke's Drift Test match in 1914 jumps out of the history books as a tale of valour when a British team, reduced to ten-men by injuries, beat a full-strength Australian side. The Origin has produced similar stories of daring and courage, such as Queensland's Bobby Lindner playing part of the third Origin match of '89 with a broken leg; Arthur Beetson inspiring the Maroons to victory in the first-ever Origin match in 1980 when most people said he should have been in a rocking chair; and who'll ever forget the sight of Benny Elias with his head swathed in bloody bandages leading the Blues to victory in 1992?

As for spite, there has been buckets of bad blood's worth. People would tune into the Origin back in the dark old days of the early

'80s expecting to see a pub brawl fought in footy boots. I remember as a kid tuning in to the Origin to watch the Queenslanders rumble against the Blues because I had a soft spot for the Maroons. It was all based on pity. I can still remember the days when New South Wales would field anything up to seven Canetoads in the sky-blue jersey and then send the visiting Queenslanders back home with their tails planted firmly between their legs . . . That ritual flogging changed under the Origin format when 'unknown' northerners such as Rohan Hancock, Wally Lewis, Mal Meninga, Chris Close and Colin Scott were buoyed by the inclusion of such southern-based 'names' as Beetson (Parramatta), Rod Morris (Balmain), Johnny Lang (Easts), Greg Oliphant (Balmain), Alan Smith (Norths), Graham Quinn (St George) and Kerry Boustead (Easts). It gave the Maroons a real edge and what also appeared to be an insatiable hunger for revenge against the New South Welshmen who'd kicked their butt so often in the past. There were some people who dismissed the Origin concept as a Mickey Mouse idea, but it took just one single blow to give the format immediate credibility—the instant Arthur Beetson biffed his Eels team-mate Mick Cronin. The punch was harmless enough, but it sowed the seeds for what has so far been seventeen years of civil war and, dare I say it, mate against mate.

As a kid, the impression I formed in our lounge room in East Ryde was that the Queenslanders had an aura of invincibility. They played with a passion that was clear for all to see. Blokes like Greg Dowling, Darryl Brohman, Gene Miles, Wally Fullerton-Smith and Mark Murray would put their body on the line for one another, and it seemed as though the Blues didn't take it as seriously as the Queenslanders. Even the supporters at Lang Park appeared to take the game a lot more seriously than we Sydneysiders. We'd see grabs of them during the television coverage and they looked wild. They'd drink their beer from yellow tins and they'd chant 'Bullshit . . . Bullshit . . . Bullshit!' whenever the referee's call went against them. Despite my having a soft spot for Wally and the boys, it was bloody frustrating living in the Harbour City back then. We'd see our boys get knocked over like tenpins and know Queenslanders were lapping up our misery. They dismissed us as 'Cockroaches', and back then there was no doubting the superiority you'd hear in any Queenslander's voice when he spoke about football. It's funny, but from my position on the lounge I used to shake my head at the Blues' commitment and I'd wonder why on earth they couldn't match muscle with the enemy. In my naivety I'd think if I was there I'd do this and I'd do that . . . but, mark my words, when I was given my call to arms for Rugby League's civil war I wouldn't have minded being safe and sound back at home and watching the massacre on television with Mum and Dad.

I was a willing conscript to the 1989 campaign because even though I'd represented Australia, I hadn't been given the sniff of a NSW jersey and I really felt as though I was missing something. So, it was with a great sense of pride that I lined up with the Blues and five other debutants: Mario Fenech, Ian Roberts, Brad Clyde, Laurie Daley and Chris Johns, while Johnny Cartwright and Greg Alexander were introduced to Origin football on the bench. Roberts later withdrew from the team with a groin injury and Peter Kelly, Canterbury's wild man of the front row, was named as his replacement. New coach Jack Gibson explained the number of rookies as a fresh start to the Blues Origin campaign and he said if New South Wales was going to lose the series, it may as well have been with new faces!

Queensland should have been the logical favourites because of their experience, but the punters saw it differently. Footy Tab gave them a 6.5 point start and former Test great Johnny Raper stirred passions north of Tweed Heads when he dismissed Queensland with a laugh. Writing in the *Sunday Telegraph*, Raper said, 'Dream on, cane toads . . . There are some great players in the Queensland side, but they have been up a long time . . . I reckon the final whistle will sound better than the dinner bell for some of those Maroon forwards . . . take plenty of hankies [Queensland supporters], you'll have plenty to cry about.'

Johnny should have warned us the whistle to signal time on was also the Queenslanders' dinner bell, because they devoured us in one of the most ruthless display of free-flowing football to flog us 36–6. It was Queensland's biggest win over New South Wales in forty-nine years, and we trudged off the field feeling humiliated. It was a matter of the experienced Queenslanders teaching the Blue greenhorns a lesson or two about the law of the jungle. Marty Bella threw himself at us and his fearless efforts not only secured him the Man of the Match award but they definitely helped Queensland get a roll on. It was terrible . . . As for me, who as a kid had wondered why the Blues couldn't match Queensland, I just wanted to know how we could save some face. When the Queenslanders opened up and scored 18 points in a ten-minute onslaught, we were gone ... physically, mentally and emotionally. Some people have said once we realised we had no hope of winning we lost the plot altogether, and I can't disagree. Little Allan Langer, Queensland's artful dodger, tormented us. The Ipswich elf was like Mary's little lamb, because everywhere the ball went Langer was sure to go. And even when we looked out at the crowd his image haunted us because 20 000 people were wearing Allan Langer masks!

It was a terrible initiation to the Origin cauldron. When the selectors met to try to salvage the second match they chopped six players, and I was among the casualties. It hurt to be dropped— actually, it made me feel filthy—but it was embarrassing just to be a witness to the second NSW humiliation when an injury-ridden Queensland side defied enormous odds to win the match 16–12. Critics called it the most embarrassing of losses. The Maroons were reduced to twelve men when Allan Langer (fractured ankle), Mal Meninga (fractured eye socket), Paul Vautin (elbow injury), Michael Hancock (shoulder) and Bob Lindner (broken leg) were dragged from the fray. We should have won but I credit the leadership of Wally Lewis for holding the thin Queensland line together ... everything he did turned to gold.

While the '89 series was an embarrassment for NSW Rugby League, it helped develop a more determined spirit to the Origin series. We'd been happy to simply compete in the series, but the humiliations fostered a great desire to put the Maroons back in their place. We 'stole' some of their ideas, such as organising a team camp and placing a much greater emphasis on team spirit, which helped to make a more level playing field. One person who I credit for doing a lot of work in that regard is Phil Gould, because he honed in on the need for spirit and camaraderie.

Under Gould the NSW side has become a lot more focused on that and the art of winning. Our first few days in camp are spent bending the elbow at the bar and one of the most popular aspects of the experience in 1993 was when we played a round of 'pub golf' in the Rocks, down by Sydney Harbour. The idea behind it was to go into a bar and try and play the par—which could be up to five schooners—before moving on to the next drinking hole. Pub golf is rather competitive, and as is the case in any major tournament the leading player wears a green (spray) jacket to the next hole. Me, I'm a hack golfer at the best of times, and my efforts in pub golf were just as ordinary as my air swings on the green, but it was a lot of fun trying to keep up with the cracking pace set by such blokes as Chris Johns and Craig Salvatori.

One of the real highlights of being part of the Origin team was our late-night singalongs at the Holiday Inn at Coogee. Gus would give Tony the piano man the nod and we'd belt out our renditions of such hits as 'Tenterfield Saddler' and 'Leaving on a Jet Plane' well into the early hours of the morning. The singing was crook, but the spirit it generated was great. I'm adamant that if you're prepared to sing in public with a group of blokes and not be embarrassed then you'll pretty much survive anything together.

Under Gould, the feeling in the dressing room just before battle has become a lot more intense. Blokes are revved right up, and by the time you leave the tunnel for the playing field it feels as though someone could hit you over the head with an axe handle and it wouldn't stop you from doing your duty. Indeed, the feeling under Gould is a world away from the time when Ted Glossop was coach of the 1988 City Origin side and he asked if any of us had last-minute questions. Well, I was pretty clear on what was expected of me but in real schoolboy fashion our veteran prop Peter Tunks stuck his hand up and asked, 'Ted, do you think I should fake my orgasms?' It brought the house down. State of Origin, however, is far too serious for that behaviour and about the only funny thing I can readily recall before a game was the night we played in front of 87 161 people at the Melbourne Cricket Ground when one member of the crowd, a shapely young lady, decided to streak. In my pumped-up state I wasn't taking much notice of the crowd, but I saw Glenn Lazarus smirking at something and when I followed his gaze I got the best eyeful of this girl. Lee-Anne will kill me for admitting this, but my concentration was diverted for a few delightful seconds. The Melbourne newspapers described the girl as perhaps the highlight of the match because our 14–0 win over the Maroons was quite a dour event. Unfortunately for the Victorian sports fraternity we were there to win, not make friends.

In saying that, however, I believe the intensity of the Origin has dropped right off in recent seasons and in my opinion that is because of the formation of the Brisbane Broncos. A lot of the old hatred seems to have gone out of the games, and I think Newcastle's Robbie O'Davis's accusation that the star-studded Canetoads of '96 lacked the same passion as the underdogs of '95 says plenty.

One of my great regrets was being overlooked for the '96 series. Gus had left me with the impression that I'd be called upon after I played in the City Origin game. Unfortunately the call never came, and I guess when my name wasn't called out it killed off any chance of my getting another sniff of battle in the State of Origin war. Like all old soldiers I often think of my time in the front line and a few random thoughts are of Paul Harragon and Marty Bella going toe-to-toe in an old-fashioned dust-up; Harragon smashing Gary Larson with a massive hit which nearly snapped the blond Queenslander in half; my lining Steve Jackson up and creaming him with one of my best-ever tackles; Allan Langer potting what was probably the only field goal he's ever attempted to give Queensland a 5–4 win in 1992; the atmosphere of playing at Lang Park and knowing they'd love to have your balls for breakfast. It really was the ultimate form of football combat.

THE KANGAROO KID

CHAPTER 11

My biggest disappointment as a member of the Australian Rugby League team wasn't losing two games to Great Britain at Wembley, but the day we played Wigan on the 1994 Kangaroo tour and their crazy forward Barrie McDermott floored me with what can only be called an evil elbow. While Bozo Fulton was to later compliment the team for not retaliating with any rough stuff, I felt let down by the boys. If that elbow had been done back in 1990, blokes like Blocker and Mark Geyer would have given McDermott an all-Aussie knuckle sandwich. The blow knocked me senseless, and I'd have felt much better had one of the 'Roos taken the law into his own hands. I guess the 'turn the other cheek' approach at Central Park that sunny Pommy afternoon is consistent with the new philosophy that drives the modern game.

I have always taken a great pride in representing Australia in battle. Most blokes play top grade football to either win a premiership or play international football, and I have many fond memories of wearing the green and gold colours. Unfortunately, when I was first given my spurs eleven years ago I failed to make the most of the opportunity. The selectors couldn't be accused of not trying to give me a leg-up: I was named in the fifteen-man 'scout' party that played the gritty PNG Kumuls at Port Moresby before we headed off to Great Britain and I was on the bench for the first Test in England. But somewhere along the way I lost the plot in the Old Dart. Instead of developing my hunger to pressure the bushy-bearded Noel Cleal and Queensland's Bryan Niebling, I was content to feed my face with those famous English breakfasts of sausages, bacon, baked beans, black pudding and lashings of heavily buttered toast. I was like the monster who ate northern England. I went on a feeding frenzy—and I paid a hefty price for my appetite. My weight ballooned by a whopping 8 kilos and I felt every one of them whenever I played for 'F Troop' in the midweek games against the Pommie club teams. It wasn't until I came home to Australia that I fully realised how great a chance I'd let slip through my fingers, and it hit me pretty hard.

The 'Roo experience was a huge eye-opener for me, however, because apart from living alongside some of the game's greatest players for two-and-a-bit months, there were so many new and wonderful experiences—such as our three-day trip to Papua New Guinea. Stepping off the aeroplane in the stifling heat of Port Moresby was an experience akin to being a member of the Beatles. Thousands of people were standing behind a 2 metre barbed-wired fence and they were greeting us with deafening cheers. As we made our way to the terminal we were called the *numba wun warriors* by our army of fans. Some locals offered their hero a special word or two of praise, such as 'Garry Jack . . . Tiger!', 'Wally, King Wally!', 'Crusher, him got big beard, Cleal' and to Chris Mortimer they asked, 'Louie, where is your brother?' It was a powerful Rugby League experience. Even though I was still wet behind the ears then, I could tell how much the game meant to these people. It was, and still is, their heart and soul, and it was very humbling to be the subject of their devotion.

As one of the less experienced Kangaroos, I expected our itinerary to centre around numerous tough training sessions and heavy team talks for the Test. You can imagine how amazed I was when the old heads dumped their gear in the hotel lobby and headed straight for the bar to refresh themselves with a few frosty ales. After a few hours' drinking Wally and Crusher decided it was time to beat the heat by swimming in the hotel's pool, and I think that was regarded as a training session! Indeed, I recall my stint in PNG as a cruisy couple of days. Outside of the game, the only time we really strained our muscles was when our mini-bus broke down on the way to an official function. We had to push the bus a few hundred metres before it would start again, and the hundreds of locals who stood by on the side of the street applauded our effort every inch of the bloody way.

The scenes outside the Lloyd Robson Oval on the day of the Test were also something completely different from anything I'd ever seen then or now. The gates swung open at 8.30 am and the oval was a sea of humanity within half an hour as the punters tried to secure a decent seat. Such is the fanaticism of the New Guineans that thousands of people milled about the gates happy to simply soak up the atmosphere of the match listening to the cheers of the massive crowd. We also absorbed the sights and sounds of the historic meeting. It was something of a modern-day adventure to be confronted by ochre-smeared warriors from the Southern Highlands dancing to the beat of tom-tom drums throughout the game. While the mob oohed and aahhed our efforts I could only shake my head in disbelief as I sat on the bench next to coach Don Furner: hanging one-handed from scaffolding and palm trees around the ground were hundreds of people whose love for the game was so strong they were prepared to risk a broken neck for a peek at the Kangaroos!

The Kumuls gave them plenty to cheer. They settled their nerves after coming face to face with their Australian heroes and played quite courageously. Their skipper, Tony Kila, played well at half-back and he turned us around quite a few times with some carefully placed kicks which knocked the stuffing out of we big blokes. Another local hero who made an impression on the green and gold machine was hard-running centre Bal Namapo, who wasn't scared to charge into our line despite being a good foot shorter than most of our blokes. Despite their efforts, we won the game 62–12 and I thoroughly enjoyed my twenty-odd minutes on the flint-hard surface. It was brilliant stuff, and seeing the looks of appreciation on the fans' faces as we walked around the ground to wave at them only added to the occasion.

From tropical PNG we headed to the bitterly cold north of England where we made the sixth floor of the Dragonara Hotel in Leeds our home—and it was a place for only the brave because plenty of atrocities went on there. Games of indoor cricket were played in the corridors, there were rumbles, pretend world champion wrestling bouts, and, if I remember correctly, there was also a game of drunken touch football played between some members of 'F Troop' towards the end of our stay. Just as was the case in PNG, the locals welcomed us with open arms, and we played Wigan before a chanting and ranting crowd of 30 000! The atmosphere was electric and it was generated by the fanaticism with which the Central Park crowd worshipped Wigan. But where the New Guineans were happy to throw their support behind the Aussies, the Wiganers bayed for our blood. We scraped home 26–18 but it set the scene for our following in the footsteps of the 1982 'Roos, who marched through Great Britain undefeated. Our tour highlighted the differences between the Aussie game and the European version. Most of us were far too fit and fast for the Brits and we had very little difficulty overcoming their opposition.

I haven't forgotten the disgust I felt four years later on the 1990 tour when I was gouged in the club match against Widnes, and I was disappointed former Kiwi Test star Kurt Sorenson was the man who was nabbed for what ranks as the lowest act on the field. He pleaded his innocence, saying the whole thing was an accident, and while that may have been so I left the field with what was diagnosed as a scratch across the clear part of my eye and the cornea. Many of the boys responded to my injury by adding plenty of sting in their tackles, and Blocker was sinbinned for thumping someone.

As you can imagine, not all of the tour was life-and-death stuff. There was plenty of time for fun. I remember some of our adventures centred around our modes of private transport—rust buckets that were just a spanner's throw away from the scrap heap. For some, such as Wally Lewis, it was a huge step down from the luxuries they were used to back home. 'The King' drove what was then a state-of-the-art Nissan 300ZX, but in England he was reduced to driving 'The Workhorse', which was really a beaten-up old brown Saab. Hell, they hammered that jalopy and by the time Wally and his crew had finished with it, it was in no condition to enter even a smash-up derby. The one I had shares in was not much better . . . I couldn't begin to tell you what it was in its previous life except it had four tyres and one door that could open. It lapped up petrol like a good-time girl does champagne, while water gushed through the radiator like Victoria Falls in Zimbabwe. Thank goodness water was free, because had we been forced to pay by the gallon we'd have been bankrupt. It sometimes took four or five buckets to fill up that radiator! Simply making a destination in our heap was considered a tremendous triumph—getting home was a bonus. In 1990, however, I chipped in to buy an old bomb with Benny Elias and a few others and I was surprised to go out to the car park of our hotel in Manchester to see Benny's family driving off in it. And, come to think of it, it was the last I ever saw of the car after that . . .

During the '86 tour fellow constable and Kangaroo Phil Daley and I met a few Leeds Railway police officers, and it was something of a surprise for us to learn they didn't carry guns. They wielded only a baton and carried a two-way radio which allowed them to call for reinforcements in the event of any serious strife. I reckon Terry Lamb was lucky the wallopers weren't about the day we were in the world famous Madame Tousade's wax museum in London because they'd have chucked him in the clink for attempted murder. It was 'Baa' at his best. We were in the sports section of the museum among some familiar faces when we spied such cricketing greats as Ian Botham and Vivian Richards. Baa, the cheeky bugger, saw a great opportunity for a laugh. He slipped under the barrier and stared straight ahead when he saw an elderly English lady and her husband walk into the room. Anyway, as the old duck looked closer at the Australian Rugby League emblem on his tracksuit, the pint-sized prankster yelled 'BOOOOOO!' and I fair dinkum thought the poor woman was going to keel over. Baa was brilliant for team morale and he played in every tour game. He also taught Penrith's whiz-kid, Greg Alexander, a trick or two about the value of backing up the ball carrier. By the end of the tour Brandy was given an insight into support play and he returned to the foot of the Blue Mountains west of Sydney a much better player.

I toured Great Britain in 1990 and '94, and by doing so I was one of only a few forwards to have ever achieved that honour. There were some great moments on and off the field but, without doubt, the most inspiring few seconds of those many weeks of football was the brilliantly sunny day when Ricky Stuart and Mal Meninga combined to save the Ashes from falling into the Poms' hands in the second Test of the '90 campaign. We'd been done over in the first Test at Wembley 19–12 before 52 000 delirious Pommie spectators and plenty of Englishmen thought *this* time they had the firepower to end Australia's dominance. The Poms had done their homework for Wembley and they kept us on the back foot with an astute kicking game—and with a ball they'd caked in bloody Vaseline! By full-time they ended our unbeaten run of thirty-seven games on British soil with a comprehensive win. Hanley played a huge game but we Aussies reckoned the whistle-happy French referee Alain Sablayrolles played an even bigger role.

Sablayrolles—or 'Salad Rolls', as we nicknamed him—was a real hands-on ref and that was nearly to his own detriment when I felt a hand on my shoulder during the Test. I turned around ready to throw a punch at what I believed was a would-be assailant. And to tell you the truth, I even considered giving the Frenchman a good shove to let him know we didn't appreciate him manhandling us, but thankfully I thought better of it. The drama that would have followed wouldn't have justified a split-second of aggro. However, not even Sablayrolles could rort us at Old Trafford when Ricky, playing in his first game for Australia as a half-back, cut loose when the score was locked at 10–all and the timekeeper was about to press the full-time buzzer. I was jogging up as a mid-field decoy when Ricky dummied his way through the Pommies' line and with Andrew Ettingshausen supporting him on his left wing he kept the Poms in two minds. But then Big Mal came from nowhere to take the ball and tearaway for a great try to give us a 14–10 win in the Test some critics called the most important for any Australian team in twelve years. I screamed myself hoarse shouting 'Go Mal, go' as he tore the heart out of the Brits with a try that will long be remembered as one of the game's great moments. As we walked from the turf I felt there was no way we wouldn't retain the Ashes, and thank goodness, my gut feeling was spot-on.

My main memory of our 14–0 victory in the third Test is that of my smashing Ellery with a few good body checks, but true to form Ellery just picked himself up and played his best for the Mother Country. And I learned from a fellow forward why Australia has called England the Mother Country for so many years—and it has nothing to do with colonial ties. 'It's because the frigging joint is full of bastards, mate . . . it's the Mother Country to millions of illegitimate so-and-sos!'

In France on the '90 tour we had a great time escaping the boredom by playing Big Men versus Little Men rumbles in the forests. The little blokes were anyone who weighed under 95 kilos and they took the fight to us—squirrel grips and all. Their 'Braveheart' was Kevin Walters who put in a blinder, and his throw on Mark

Carroll would have put Jean Claude Van Damme to shame! He *mashed* Spud Carroll. We didn't cross Van Damme on our travels but we did meet Kevin Costner while he was filming the movie *Robin Hood* in the ancient walled city of Carcassone. A lot of blokes complained about the language barrier in France and perhaps Costner was happy to meet up with a group of blokes who could speak English, despite our 'funny' accents. Anyway, he braved the bitterly cold winds that cut through us all to get his first taste of Rugby League—Australia vs Roussillon—and we cruised home 38–9. He was one of the thousand fans who turned out, and I enjoyed explaining the differences between Rugby League and American Football. He seemed a decent bloke, and much to our surprise he partied on with the boys into the early hours of the morning.

Two players who paid the price for partying hard were poor old Penrith stalwart Johnny Cartwright and Brisbane's Kevin Walters, because when they suffered an attack of the munchies they tried to force their way into an eatery. Instead of being cared for by a waiter, they were greeted by a terrified owner who thought the drunk Aussies were thieves and he sprayed them with mace. Carty copped the full brunt of it in his eyes, and with Kevin acting as his eye dog they stumbled down the street trying to get away from the restaurant owner and his mates and fearful a bashing was on the cards. They took refuge in an alleyway and as they tried to clear their eyes of the chemicals two local police officers stumbled upon them. Kevvy handed one of them a fistful of francs and pleaded for him to get them a cab but the copper pocketed the cash and told them to push off. I still don't know how they managed to do it but they made their way back to the hotel and were given emergency treatment by our team doctor, Nathan Gibbs. John recovered from his eye injuries but I don't think he ever felt quite the same about Mark Geyer again who he trusted to lead him around while his eyes were patched up with Felix Fly-type pads, but he'd end up in the women's toilets and other embarassing situations!

Without a doubt the best gee up was in France the night we stumbled across a bar which had a piano with a dummy pianist in front of it. If a button was pressed from behind the bar the dummy's hand would appear to tinkle the ivories. It was a godsend and a few of us hid the dummy and arranged for the barman to press the button and make it look as if I was playing the piano when Spud

Carroll walked in. It was cruel because as I played everything from classical tunes to the Beetles poor old Spud shook his head and urged me to give up football and concentrate on music. Yeah, I felt a bit of a cur when I put my hands up on top of the piano and shouted, 'Look Spud no hands!' as the music kept playing.

Spud wasn't the only bloke to be made a gig of. In the Test against the Frogs I thought I heard the crowd chanting *Sirro* over and over again. I did the right thing and waved at my army of 'fans' as a humble but genuine show of thanks. My melon turned a bright shade of red, however, when the Frog coach finally gave their hero, the black winger Cyrille Pons, a run.

The '94 tour, the campaign in which the Super League threat became a reality, was a major disappointment. I was dropped after our first Test loss at Wembley and was given no real opportunity to force my way back into the side. It was a tragedy because I started the tour off as the skipper of the Australian team that ran rings around Cumbria at Workington and it was one of my greatest honours, to skipper Australia. I was totally stuffed as to why I was axed after our shock defeat at Wembley. It is still a great mystery to me. Lee-Anne had made the long trip from Sydney with baby Curtis to get an idea of what the 'Roo tours were all about and sadly, while I'd have loved for her to see me in a few more Tests, she had to be content with seeing me play against the club teams. It was ironic that on my first Kangaroo trip I didn't really appreciate the opportunity I'd been given, and on my third and final trip I worked overtime to try to fight my way back to the top. Life's funny like that.

Wembley has been cruel to me on two occasions, but it is still a huge buzz to play there. It has a real aura of tradition and pomp and pageantry. Every player participating in a match there is given a six page booklet on what is expected of them, and apart from pretty much mapping out every minute of the afternoon it almost reads as a legal document: 'The teams, referees and touch judges will be in the tunnel, prepared to enter the arena at 2.33 pm. At 2.34 pm the team shall line up in numerical order behind their respective captain and on receipt of a signal from a member of the Rugby Football League staff standing at the entrance to the arena the manager of the Australian team will lead his team onto the arena . . . ' It was too bad the booklet didn't tell us how to go about beating the twelve-man Brit side, because they just got a roll on.

Even though the scoreline read 8–0 the Poms hammered us, and the ancient Welsh fullback Jonathon Davies sealed our fate when he beat Brett Mullins's desperate tackle to score a memorable try. We should have had the game wrapped up when the Lions skipper Shaun Edwards was dismissed for his high hit on Brad Clyde—it was a shocker—but as it turned out the pressure was placed on *us* and we didn't handle it at all. I was happy to be over there for the tour, but knowing I wasn't going to feature in the last two Tests to defend the Ashes took some gloss off the campaign for me. But I was as proud as punch that Mal bowed out a winner by leading Australia to a 74–0 Test win against a hapless French rabble.

I have been blessed to play in successful Ashes defences and World Cup triumphs and my favourite tour for so many reasons was the trip to New Zealand in 1989. I made the side after being dropped from the NSW squad following our flogging in the first Origin game, and plenty of critics were squealing when I was selected. They called it a joke. Coach Bobby Fulton set me right though when he said he appreciated my efforts in our World Cup win over New Zealand in '88 and he was sure I could do the same in the three Test match series. The football was nice and tough but some of the main memories I have of that tour was how Blocker and Sammy Backo kept us all in good humour with their front-row logic. Before we'd go out on the town Steve would ask Sam, 'How do I look mate, do I look okay?' To which smooth Sammy would say, 'Block, you look a million dollars. What about me?' And I must admit I came close to vomiting when Roachy said, 'Sam, you look handsome. You'll break many hearts tonight.' It was also no joke the day we were all talking about the Maori names given to places like Otago, Rotorua and the like when Sam said, 'Look, there's one on that shop front—Take-away. It must be pronounced Tak-e-wayee!' Block took it upon himself to correct his upfront mate and he pointed out it was a milk bar. Steve couldn't afford to be smug for too long, however, because I was sitting near him the day when someone commented on how nice the bacon was at breakfast. Block fired back as if he was talking to a dodo, 'Well, why wouldn't the bacon be friggin' tasty? They have 200 million sheep here!' Mmm, it was always an adventure.

I strung together some of my best performances on the international front on that tour and I earned plenty of rave reviews which silenced the knockers. Our first Test win was a beauty. The

As a rookie
I always did my
best to feed the
ball to the likes of
Blocker and Benny

Action Photographics

Sometimes football can be akin to running into
brick walls.   Action Photographics

It was once a great thing to have a bad hair day...

Action Photographics

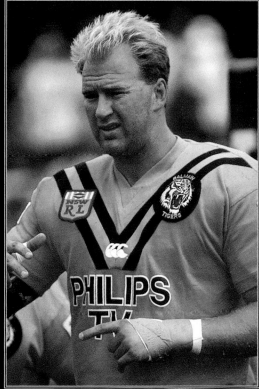

Taking on Newcastle is never any fun.

Action Photographics

I loved barging through
the Englishmen.

Action Photographics

Television commentator Graeme
Hughes quizzes me about what
kind of washing powder Lee-
Anne uses.

Action Photographics

It is so important to try and make
that extra yard in attack.
Action Photographics

Employing some strong-arm tactics
against the Rabbitohs

SPLAT! Canberra's Jason Croker has
his nose flattened by my thigh.
Action Photographics

I needed the ice pack for my sore head after Brad Mackay and I were treated to the best of Terry Hill's jokes during a City-Country Origin Match.

Bracing myself for impact against Canterbury

(opposite) Looking to offload against the Sea Eagles

Getting a worms eye view of
the action

Australian trainer Brian Hollis gives me
a helping hand during the 1994
Kangaroo tour.

Andrew Varley

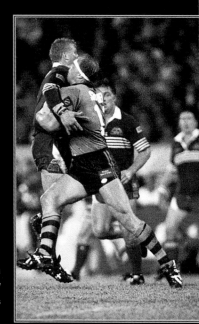

Taking part in the State of Origin
smash up Derby

Action Photographics

On the fly against Great Britain
Sportsphoto Agency (Richard Sellers / Sportsphoto)

Trying to break the
Manly line...
Action Photographics

Part of the hard work
which is involved in being
a first-grader

Feeling every bit the old man tiger in 1997
ABC Stills / Ludwik Dabrowski

Getting a pass away to my support in the opening match of the '97 season, my 200th first-grade game for Balmain
ABC Stills / Ludwik Dabrowski

Kiwis, led by debutant Brendan Tuuta, tried to bash us out of the game. Tuuta went ballistic and he was lucky not to be sent off for kneeing Paul Vautin in the head. He was penalised four times in the first half and with each penalty he conceded, Tuuta made his country's job of beating us even tougher. Actually, every one of our first 20 points was the result of undisciplined Kiwi play and one person who was unhappy with Tuuta's performance was former New Zealand coach Graeme Lowe. He said it was a pity Tuuta didn't react to the situation properly: 'It really annoys me to see young blokes pull on a Kiwi jersey and then go around trying to decapitate the opposition!'

As for me, I enjoyed the conditions over there. Apart from making some good hits on the New Zealanders, it was brilliant to run onto some Blocker passes in the two Tests I played in (I missed the third through injury), and some people even pinpointed the Balmain partnership as a key to our winning the Trans-Tasman trophy. I won the Player's Match ball at Christchurch and was awarded the Man of the Match award at Rotorua—and that was something special. As a player who loves representing his country, I can say there is nothing like the green and gold fever . . . it makes your heart beat faster to hear your name read out and it inspires you to lift yourself above any injury. It is something every footballer should bust a gut to savour, because it is the ultimate.

FRIENDS AND CRITICS

CHAPTER 12

Laurie Nicholls is a mad Balmain fan, though some people reckon he's just plain mad—and with a capital M. If you've ever watched Balmain play then chances are you've seen him in action. He's the snowy-haired bloke and no matter what the weather he'll religiously wear a Balmain training singlet. He spends half the game shadow-boxing and chanting 'Tiger . . . Tiger . . . Tigerrrrrssss'. He's a wool classer by trade, but he constantly butchers the English language with such things as his little rhymes for each player, such as 'Ellery eats celery' and 'David Brooks destroys good looks!' Above all, however, Laurie is a loyal Balmain boy who loves his club so much he travels all the way from Springwood in the Blue Mountains to attend Balmain games all over the country. The man is a freak, and adding to his charm is the fact he believes there is no such thing as a bad Tiger. I'd advise anyone who wants to suggest otherwise to forget it—Laurie will spend all night chewing you out!

I grew quite concerned when I heard stories that Laurie, a veteran of the old Jimmy Sharman boxing tents that travelled to showgrounds all around the country, had thrown a few punches on behalf of Blocker and myself when stirrers took to criticising us. They were probably only half joking when they wrote Blocker off as a meathead and dismissed me as a cat, but good ol' Laurie took it personally and he sent schooners of frothy beer, tables and chairs crashing as he sorted out the renegade. When I heard of Laurie's hardline approach, I begged him to cut out the rough stuff and explained it wasn't worth all the hassle. I also pointed out Roachy and I were big and ugly enough to look after ourselves. True to his form though, Laurie said, 'Sirro, no bludger knocks me mates!'

Bearing that in mind there are a few blokes fortunate not to have my mate Laurie on their cases because I've copped some heavy duty serves over the years from so called experts and numerous bar-room critics. The most popular theory, and one that has plagued me for years, is that I'd play my heart out in the representative matches but I'd drop back to cruise control when it came to the weekly grind of club football. These experts are the same people who said Australia's great boxer of the '70s and early '80s, Tony Mundine, had a glass jaw and they're also the ones who bagged Australian Test cricket skipper Mark Taylor when he lost his form. They're knockers, and unfortunately Australia seems to be full of them. Naturally, I refute the allegations they made about me not trying for Balmain because I know within myself I put plenty on the line for the Tigers. I've suffered some terrible injuries over the years as a legacy of my commitment to Balmain and my theory is a player won't ever get injured if he's out on the field bludging.

Whenever I've sat down to try and work out where the criticism about my supposed lack of intensity stemmed from, I pinpoint my rookie days when I found it hard to override the calls of the senior guys. As a result, the many workhorses in the Tigers pack would run the ball up which meant out of *some* sets of six I wouldn't be involved in *one* play because the other blokes were getting to the ball first. I think most rookies go through a stage like that until they find their place in the team, and I was fortunate to have a coach such as Frank Stanton and some solid team-mates who helped guide me through that initiation with a minimum of fuss.

Another factor from my early days which I guess some people have held against me is that because I've always been a pretty big unit it takes quite a few weeks for me to get back into the swing of things ... but it can be quite difficult to get that through some people's skulls. One person who I blame for lumbering me with the tag as a player who didn't put in during the club scene is former St George and Wests coach, Roy Masters, who writes about sport for the *Sydney Morning Herald*. He seemed to think I didn't show enough commitment in the week-to-week grind of the premiership and while it was a pretty rough call, it was one many people took to heart. Apart from my old cobber Laurie Nicholls the allegations also annoyed another club stalwart, our old conditioner, Les Hobbs. Hobbsy believed my biggest problem was people in the grandstands expected way too much from me because of my dimensions, and he told *Queensland Rugby League Star*:

> Because Sirro is such a big man, everyone wants to pick on him. He has to perform week in, week out, simply because he stands out so much.
>
> But the truth of the matter is that Paul is a marked man before he goes out onto the field . . . more times than not, he's belted before he gets the ball. And the reason for that is simple. The opposition knows how dangerous he is and they do things like that to cushion his impact.

I don't worry about what the critics have to say about me these days but there was a time when I took their assessments to heart . . . and it hurt me. When my name was read out as part of the 1992 Australian Test side to play Great Britain, it was greeted with an avalanche of criticism from all sections of the media and other experts who looked as though they couldn't tell the difference between a fire engine and a football. I admit that in the lead-up to my selection for the Ashes series my form wasn't the best, but I hung in there for the five weeks before the first Test and things came together. In the final Origin match won by New South Wales 16–4 I played pretty well, and when I was replaced by Craig Salvatori with ten minutes to go it was nice to get a bit of an ovation from the crowd. But all that went out the window when the selectors gave me the nod for the green and gold, and it was one time when I couldn't turn the other cheek. I told Tim Prentice of the *Daily Telegraph Mirror* that enough was enough and I wanted a break from the baggers. 'It has almost become fashionable to pay out on me,' I said. 'Every footballer has his share of critics but some of them have been downright unfair towards me.'

Nowadays I have simply accepted that some people are always going to have a shot at me no matter how I play, so I just play a straight bat to it. The only time I have ever phoned a journalist to bellyache about an article was in 1995 when the *Daily Telegraph*'s Ray Kershler wrote in his column that he couldn't understand why I was complaining about being paid $75 000 to remain with the ARL while reserve graders were getting more than me. Kershler suggested I should be grateful for whatever came my way and I took that as a bit of a slap in the face. To his credit, however, he did point out in his following week's column that I wasn't happy with his comments.

On the other hand, I'm told by a journalist who covered the French leg of the 1994 Kangaroo tour that the universal feeling towards me in France is somewhat different from that in Australia. 'Sirro,' he gushed, 'You're a legend over there. The Frogs were dirty when you went back to Australia early!' In light of that perhaps my comeback line to any future criticism should be, 'Well, I'm a legend in France—what the hell are you?' Who knows, maybe that might shut a few people up once and for all.

MONEY MATTERS

CHAPTER 13

I'm not a greedy bloke, not by a long shot. There have been times in my career when I could have squeezed more money out of Balmain, but it didn't seem the right thing to do. I've never believed Rugby League is merely an avenue to make money and without wanting to sound corny, the game has always meant much more to me than that. After all, this is the sport that caused me to sulk as a kid whenever heavy rain forced my junior matches to be postponed; this is the game from which I've forged lifetime friendships; this is the game that has taught me a lot about myself; and this is the game that has afforded me the honour of representing Australia. Of course it hasn't all been beer and skittles, and Rugby League has also been a mean bitch to me on different occasions. I've suffered plenty of disappointments, such as losing *two* grand finals, being dropped from representative teams and then suffering heartbreaking injuries. In the grand scheme of things those inconveniences are merely a pimple on the face of a great love.

However, I'm worried by what can only be described as a mercenary approach by many of the younger blokes coming through the ranks. For example, I find it unbelievable to learn junior representative players are demanding up to $30 000 a season. It's bloody ludicrous and I'm afraid by going along with it chief executives are sending out all the wrong messages. I don't lay all the blame on the kids—they're having it drummed into their heads by managers, advisers and even the media to get in and make a quick killing. They're being told no-one will give a toss about them when they finish their careers, and I've found that talk has fostered an 'us against them' approach when it comes to dealing with their club's management. Also, I think some rather ordinary players are developing over-inflated egos, but that is a different story.

There are many advantages involved in being a full-time footballer: it allows a player to learn his trade better; he doesn't have such unwanted pressures as juggling jobs with football commitments; and he can focus on fulfilling his potential. Most players coming through the ranks, though, believe the term 'professional' means selling their soul to the highest bidder and damning the consequences! I guess my thoughts on club loyalty have been coloured by coming through the grades with a tight-knit bunch of guys who were almost like a family. Balmain had such a great spirit back then. The majority of our players cut their teeth in the local juniors and most of us grew up alongside each other. If we didn't know one another from school then we were acquainted by playing in the junior competition or the Balmain representative teams. That helped develop a tremendous team spirit, and once we made grade it made us a strong force. To a man we'd get a lot of pride from reading the *Rugby League Week* Player Polls in the mid-1980s and learning Balmain not only ranked as one of the sides our opponents loathed playing but that they regarded Leichhardt Oval as the nearest thing possible to a snake pit.

Our feeling for the place was often utilised by the then chief executive Keith Barnes when he negotiated the players' contracts at the end of each season.

I remember he'd appeal to my sense of loyalty and apart from singing the club's praises he'd add an extra coat of gloss by saying such things as I was *lucky* to be playing alongside Steve Roach who was feeding me so many good passes. Barnesy would say 75 per cent of my tries came from short Blocker Roach passes—and he was spot on! I laughed my head off when I learned Keith told Benny Elias he was *lucky* to have good ball-runners such as me and Blocker because *we* made *him* look good. And when Roachy walked in to haggle and barter he too was fed a similar 'lucky-for-you' yarn. There's no doubt we could all have made more money at other clubs, but Blocker,

Benny, Kerry Hemsley, David Brooks, Wayne Pearce and the other boys could see more at Leichhardt than just dollar signs.

Mind you, the temptation was always there to take the money and run. In 1986 I received a massive offer to join Souths, and the kind of money their chief executive Terry Parker was talking about was huge for back then—it was worth close to $50 000 and made the $8000 sign-on I received from Balmain at the beginning of the season look like a pittance. There was also the added attraction of playing alongside the likes of such toughnuts as Mario Fenech, Les Davidson, Craig Coleman and Ian Roberts. Apart from my feeling of belonging at Balmain there were incentives in my contract that made my being a Tiger worthwhile, but they were dependent upon my performing and I had no trouble with that. I was happy to back my own ability then, and I still am.

The latest generation of kids are getting set-for-life deals and I fear there's a danger some might think they can afford to sit back and not try as hard since no matter how they play they're guaranteed their money at the end of the day. Obviously, I'm not that grumpy an old man to suggest *every* kid will fall into that comfort zone. So long as footy is played there'll always be kids with personal pride in their performance . . . they'll always stand out. But I reckon we'll see a few more lazy kids come through the system.

I must also admit my decision to remain with the Tigers in '86 was made amid the emotion of the club's annual presentation night. It was a funny time because there'd been speculation in the press that I was set to join Souths or Manly, and a few of the Leichhardt diehards weren't happy. Any chance I had of migrating to Redfern or Brookvale vanished when I stood on the stage to accept my awards as Balmain's Rookie of the Year and the Player's Player. I was overwhelmed by the occasion, and I dug my own grave when I announced, 'I'll be here next year!' To this day I'm sure that huge sound of something breaking at the back of the auditorium that night was my poor bank manager's heart.

One of the most extraordinary meetings I've ever participated in took place when I was summoned to the office of Australia's richest man, Kerry Packer. He wanted to ask just one question, 'Son, do you want to play for Manly?' Packer had thrown his support behind the Sea Eagles in 1986 because of his strong friendship with their coach, Bobby Fulton. Manly had embarked on an aggressive recruiting campaign and through Packer they'd made massive offers to Queensland heroes Wally Lewis and Gene Miles to add some extra zing to their backline. When the QRL counteracted with an even better deal to keep Wally and Gene, the Sea Eagles then reset their sights on other targets, and I was among them. Packer's overture was extremely tempting. I mean, just having Kerry Packer, a man who had bought and sold television and radio stations, try to woo me was a compliment. It could have been so easy to just say, 'Where do I sign, KP?' But I didn't. When push came to shove, I couldn't leave my mates . . . just as Wayne Pearce couldn't when he met Jack Gibson in the Parramatta car park to discuss a possible future in the blue and gold of the Eels. And if that makes us silly in this new age of get-what-you-can, I'll wear a dunce's hat and sit in the corner.

Apart from the madness of 1986, the closest I came to leaving Balmain was in 1994—ironically my testimonial year—when I seemed set to accept a deal with either Cronulla or Easts (now Sydney City). I was twenty-nine and the Sharks offered me $240 000 while the Roosters were in the early $200s. At the time, I thought I needed a change to recharge my batteries. To be brutally honest I wasn't happy with the way Wayne Pearce was handling the job as coach of a struggling team, and I told him that to his face. So I began to search for something else, and the idea of either coming under John Lang's guidance at Cronulla or trying to help give the Roosters a bit of a kick-along appealed to me. My dealings with the Roosters hit a snag when Phil Gould left Penrith mid-season to take up the reins at Bondi. I phoned Gus to tell him I was keen to play for Easts as I had a high regard for the way he did things and Phil indicated he'd welcome me in the red, white and blue. It seemed a done deal and the *Sun-Herald*'s Greg Prichard even trumpeted the news that 'Paul Sironen will play the next two seasons with Eastern Suburbs. The deal will be completed within days . . . '

There was, however, one clause and that was Easts didn't want me to tour with the Kangaroos because they didn't want me to risk aggravating my back problem. I didn't give myself much chance of making the squad, so I agreed. After pretty much committing myself to Easts I was left waiting, and waiting, by the phone and growing more frustrated as each hour passed by. It was apparent something had gone wrong and as I tried to work out the possible scenarios, I figured maybe Phil didn't really want me there. In the end I phoned the Roosters and told them where to stick their offer. They'd screwed me about pretty badly but what angered me most of all was no-one there had the gumption to phone and tell me what was happening. Unfortunately the Easts 'deal' didn't end there because two days after I told them to shelve it their president, Nick Politis, went to the press and announced our negotiations collapsed because I didn't fit in with their future plans! 'Paul is a great player and one of the gentlemen of the game but he doesn't really fit in with our long-term plans,' he told the *Tele-Mirror*.

> Because of the money Paul is able to command we could not afford to spend that much on one player because of our salary cap commitments. I said when Phil Gould was appointed coach for next year that we would not be active in the transfer market until the 1996 season. If there are players available later this year who suit our plans we will talk to them but we have our sights set on young players whose contracts expire next year.

I was furious that Politis hadn't told the truth. I *was* initially in their long-term plans, but when they stuffed me about I called the negotiations to a halt. It was as simple as that. Meanwhile, the Cronulla administration remained active and their phone calls asking me to hurry up and give them an idea of where I was headed added extra pressure. And Balmain were also waiting in the wings . . . Lord knows I'll never forget the day I was at a luncheon with Keith Barnes and he asked me what the hell I intended to do. I told him I would probably stay and he was delighted. Indeed, Barnesy even told the Tiger's directors the good news and they set about drawing up a new contract. However, in the meantime I had a heart-to-heart with Les Hobbs and finished the chat determined to join Cronulla. It was confusing for me but it was heart attack material for Keith—he turned pale when he heard I'd had yet another change of heart! It wasn't until I had a long, deep and meaningful chat with Junior and Keith that I finally signed on the dotted line.

A friend of mine who is involved in the promotions industry reckons I deserved a kick up my big backside for not re-signing with the Tigers a week before my testimonial. He reckons there'd have been more than the 300 supporters to toast my decade at Leichhardt had I signed a new deal with the club. Maybe he was right, but it doesn't matter. That night remains one of my most treasured memories from being a member of the Balmain club . . . it was special. I guess most of those great people who were in the club's auditorium that night probably thought the function was really my farewell, but Blocker dropped a big hint concerning my future when he told the guests, 'Don't believe everything you read in the papers!' I remember it as quite an amazing night. Apart from hearing a few of my old team-mates say nice things about me, I was touched by the battlers and the diehard supporters who begged me not to leave the joint. It was an atmosphere of great affection and as I sat there getting drunk on the sentiment and the kindness of friends I guess I knew the colours I'd be playing in 1995 and beyond.

When I finally agreed to stay with Balmain, for what was then the richest deal a Tiger player had ever received, I felt a great load fall off my shoulders. It allowed me to get back to the business of just worrying about playing football. I believe a player's form is affected by the type of pressure I faced in 1994 because it is *always* on your mind. For some people, like Keith Barnes, my decision to stay with the Tigers for an amount less than what Cronulla had offered meant a lot to him, and he told the media, 'Obviously he has been under a lot of pressure and it shows that blood is a lot thicker than water. He has been at the club ten years and he wants to play for the one club for his career.'

Even Cronulla's larger-than-life football manager Shane Richardson overcame any disappointment he may have felt when he told the *Sydney Morning Herald* he could understand why I remained at Balmain, and he even suggested it was a good result for the game: 'There has been a lot of crap written lately that there's no loyalty in Rugby League, but I think that Paul Sironen proved that it does exist. I think the decision he made was a noble one . . . I think it's great for the game.'

Things weren't too warm on the homefront when I turned my back on the Sharks, and Lee-Anne refused to speak to me for a couple of days. When I fielded the Sharks offer we spent quite some time over at Cronulla looking at properties and I think Lee-Anne fell in love with the idea of a house on the water at Gunnamatta Bay or Yowie Bay. While she didn't go so far as to dump my dinner over my head, I think she toyed with the idea a few times.

The only time I've ever felt really filthy about money matters was when I was paid $75 000 'loyalty' money by the ARL at the height of the Super League war. I was happy enough until the newspapers published the amount of money Phillip Street had shelled out on horseflesh and I lagged behind such reserve graders as Scott Fulton, son of Bob, who received $100 000 for his signature. I wouldn't try to insult anyone's intelligence by saying $75 000 is something to sneeze at, it isn't, but I felt I'd been dudded by the ARL. It was as though they hadn't really budgeted for me in their recruitment plans and I was just an afterthought. I twigged something was wrong the morning the lists were published and I fielded half-a-dozen calls from journalists wanting to know my reaction. Well, I was furious. I thought I'd been misrepresented by Phillip Street when they told me I was signing a great deal. And there were a few other problems associated with the agreement, such as where I stood on the matter of playing in Super League-aligned England when my Balmain contract expired.

What added further to my frustrations was that no-one in Phillip Street seemed interested in discussing my grievances. On legal advice I had the relevant papers drawn up to take the ARL to court on the basis I was induced into signing a deal with them after receiving misrepresentation on various issues. I waited a year before threatening to take the ARL to court because I loathed the idea of dragging the game through yet another legal battle after the negative effect the courtroom dramas had on the game during the ARL–Super League war, but I was forced to move when no-one wanted to assume responsibility for my problem.

When John Quayle retired and my old Balmain mate Neil Whittaker took over, I was in a quandary. Not only did I fear the ARL was running low on funds, but I didn't think having me kicking and screaming would be all that great an initiation for the old Tiger hooker in his new job. I was happy, however, when Neil showed enough initiative to suggest we meet in his office on the eve of the 1997 Optus Cup kick-off to try to work out my problems. As I expected, he and the ARL's national premiership communications officer Geoff Carr said there was little they could do for me except guarantee I'd be free to play in England. They said because there were other players in a comparable position to mine, they could leave themselves open for similar demands. And, by the tone of their voices, it sounded as though that would push Phillip Street into total financial ruin. I didn't want that, so I just rolled my eyes and decided to drop the matter . . . it wasn't worth the drama. And, as I've already said—money, baby, it ain't everything!

ROY, HG ... AND MY LIFE AS IAN

CHAPTER 14

If laughter is the best medicine, then 'Rampaging' Roy Slaven and his sidekick HG Nelson are the two greatest things to hit the scene since penicillin. The way they lampooned Rugby League and other sports on their Triple J show, *This Sporting Life* was nothing short of brilliant, and their observations of different players always leave me in stitches ... just as they did when I first heard them back in '88.

One of the best things that has happened to me outside of Rugby League was getting dragged into their weird and wild world as 'Ian' in a soap opera they created especially for their variety show on the ABC, *Club Buggery*. It was a definite eye-opener and I find it amazing that even now, a few years after the last episode was screened, I'm still recognised as Ian by some people in the streets. Actually, one of the biggest surprises was the time we played an Origin match in Victoria and I made an appointment to see one of Australia's gun physiotherapists based in the Melbourne central business district. When the lift doors closed a well-dressed businessman looked at me in total amazement and spluttered, 'I know you ... you're Ian!' It blew me away, because this joker didn't know me as a sportsman but as a boofheaded Aussie bloke named Ian.

I remember back in 1988 I was advised to tune in to these two jokers on the radio because they pulled no punches when it came to assessing players. I took the tip, and by the time they'd signed off Wally Lewis had been dismissed as a 'joke', . . . I was known as 'Buttocks' because that was my most noticeable feature, Ian Roberts was dubbed 'Cabanossi' because he owned a delicatessen on Oxford Street, Mark Geyer became 'the Tap' because he could apparently turn the aggression on and off, and Glenn Lazarus was the 'Brick with Eyes'. I became addicted to their humour. When Roy and HG got behind the microphone, nothing was sacred. Within weeks of their first hitting the airwaves they boasted a cult audience and forged a reputation for themselves as sports experts blessed with tongues like a bullocky's lash, and legend had it their forefingers were bent out of shape from ramming them into one another's chest while stressing a point.

And they discussed *all* the big issues, such as the Tim Fischer Option—mandatory marriage for coaches. Then there was the time when the ABC and ARL were having a donnybrook about screening footy on television. The boys did some serious searching for an independent view on the ramifications of the argument and they came up with that renowned political analyst, Mr Arthur Beetson. According to Roy and HG, big Artie feared the state and federal governments could crumble as a result of the stoush and it could also jeopardise our trade relations with some countries.

I found *This Sporting Life* a great way to escape from all the life-and-death seriousness of Rugby League and I laughed myself stupid as Roy and HG reported on the supposed cross-dressing shenanigans of some tough forwards and high-profile jockeys. In between scoops and scandals they advertised their own range of goods such as a skin and hair-care range endorsed by Peter Tunks, and it was hilarious because Tunksy has the kind of face that would flatten out sandpaper! They were good at putting people in unbelievable situations.

Adding to their popularity was the fact that for the first few years nobody knew who the hell Roy Slaven and HG Nelson really were because they refused to make public appearances or pose for photographs. Their true identities were a closely guarded secret and the only publicity shot the ABC would issue of the pair was of two unidentified race-goers with their backs to the camera watching a racehorse in the mounting yard. Indeed, the question often asked by we players was, 'HG Nelson: man or myth? Rampaging Roy Slaven: myth or man?', but we lapped up their views of the sporting world with great gusto. The more we asked for them to show their faces, the happier they seemed to remain out of sight—perhaps the thought of Cabanossi, Tap, Buttocks or Brick throttling them kept them on the hop.

If what you believe in the paper is true, however, we should have been able to at least put a face to one voice, that of Rampaging Roy Slaven, the Lithgow lad who claimed to tour Great Britain with Roy Bull and the Kangaroos back in 1952. As the 1990 squad jetted off to England, Slaven told the *Sunday Telegraph*'s Mike Colman of his greatest moment: 'When word came through on the blower, it was a Sunday night like any other. I was sitting around with Mum and Dad having just put in a pretty hard game for the Lithgow Shamrocks. About half-past nine, [chairman of selectors] Ernie Hammerton was on the phone and he just said, "Roy, pack your bags son." He called me son and asked me to call him Dad, which I did—and it confused my dad no end. Not that it mattered—he was as proud as punch.' Through Colman, Slaven painted the excitement that engulfed Lithgow when it became common knowledge one of their boys had made the Kangaroo tour: 'Wherever I went the word seemed to spread before me. The porch lights would go on and out. They'd come with a beer or a Jatz, maybe with a piece of salami ... whatever they had they'd want to share, and they'd shout out, "Kangaroo, how do you feel?"'

Apparently Rampaging Roy Slaven's crowning moment was the day he and Roy Bull took on the English club team Wigan by themselves because the other Kangaroos were stuffed after a night on the tiles ... but, that's another tall story. Truth is, his 193 centimetre tall and 89 kilo alter ego, John Doyle, did play some Rugby League as a second-rower for a Catholic school team, but he's unable to recall too much success on the paddock.

'I went to the De La Salle Brothers' College and there were two religions,' he told the *Sydney Morning Herald*. 'Rugby League and Catholicism ... in that order. I played in the second row but it was a game my heart was never in. I was happier to watch rather than get winded.'

As it turned out, his upfront buddy HG Nelson, who hailed from drought-ravaged Wilcannia, was another hoaxer. HG is really a bloke from Adelaide named Greig Pickhaver and he knew enough about

Rugby League to ridicule it, the fans and the players. My association with these two scurrilous characters began in the early '90s when I was asked to endorse Roy and HG's holiday resort, 'Club Nude'. In between fits of laughter I managed to blurt out something like, 'G'day, it's Sirro here, and I've just returned from Roy and HG's Club Nude, and my batteries have been recharged.' While I'm sorry to say one lower grader at Leichhardt asked me how he should go about checking in to enjoy the sunshine at Club Nude, that skit was the beginning of a tremendous relationship. I'll never forget the scene at our wedding reception when someone played a tape Roy and HG had put together for the occasion. We had trouble hearing it over the laughter but as they reported 'live' from Room 14 at the Welcome Hotel in Rozelle—the place where Lee-Anne and I were meant to be spending our wedding night—they spoke about everything from my bad habits to the first time HG saw me play in the Balmain juniors:

> He was a kiddie who had very limited skills and very limited talent. I remember the first time I saw him I was wandering past what might have been an under-14s or a 6 stone 7 game. I was with Frank Hyde, Dud Beattie [national selector], Ron Jones [Easts boss] and Ernie Hammerton [national selector]—just the five of us. We used to do in an old-fashioned way back then what was known as talent spotting among the kiddies, so we'd wander about and that was, of course, Paul Sironen. He was a bloke who, from memory, dropped the ball on every occasion, who'd do very little in defence and who tended to run away from the ball. But I did notice he had something about him . . . the players looked to him whenever something went wrong. They'd come up and say, 'Sirro, where did we go wrong, what can we do?' The coach also conferred with Paul at half-time and I noticed—we went over and had a listen as they were having their oranges—and nobody was listening to the coach, they were listening to Sirro. He said, 'I think we've got to go forward, a bit more ball security, cherish the ball, do *something* with it whenever we've got it . . . and hit 'em so they stay hit when they've got the cherry and we'll be all right.' He was ten at the time, he was a kid with great wisdom . . . they went out and lost the game but Paul put in a blinder!'

As for our marriage the boys were at their cutting best saying, 'I think it's fair to say that had Paul not met Lee-Anne he would have been a hopeless joke to himself and his family and the whole Balmain club connection. And I think had Lee-Anne not met Paul she would have been destined to be lonely and unhappy and a bit of a joke and no-one would have spent much time talking to her or being interested in her . . .' In three minutes, the duration of their tape, they reduced the reception hall into a mass of laughter.

I was happy the boys didn't forget me when they put the cast together for *World of Ian*, and I'm extremely grateful I wasn't forced to find out what some Hollywood starlets mean by doing 'favours' on the casting couch to get their big break in acting. Instead, I was invited to lob up to the ABC studio along with former Olympic swimmer Lisa Forrest, who played Ian's love interest, Susan; former international cricketer Greg Matthews, who was Ian's best mate, Col; singers Col Joy (Ian's dad) and Ted Mulray (Bob the neighbour); SBS personality Annette Shun Wah, who played Bob's wife Angie; and footy commentator Warren Boland, who was introduced late in the series as Col's 'special' friend Pete. It was a great hoot. The episodes only went for two-and-a-bit minutes, but they took hours to complete because we often cracked up after losing the plot.

World of Ian was a tale about an ordinary bloke, his ordinary wife, his ordinary life and ordinary neighbours, and the plots had enough twists and turns to rival *Neighbours* and *Home And Away*. By the series end, Ian had lost it when he suspected Bob the neighbour was having an affair with Susan. Ian based his suspicions on finding a fishing rod under the bed and his whole life became dedicated to making Bob's life a living hell by planting marijuana on his boat and ringing the cops, ripping up Bob's mail, doing a crap on his front doorstep, super-gluing Bob's bowling balls together, and laser printing a police wanted poster of Bob, the drug dealer. In what was perhaps *World of Ian*'s most dramatic moment, Ian pinned a note on the bowling club's noticeboard which read, 'My name is Bob and if anyone wants to buy grass, coke or whores for sex then don't hesitate to bale me up at the bar or on the green. And if any pigs come looking for me tell them to get a dog up themselves.'

Apart from bringing Ian's dark side to the fore, the show also inspired some real golden moments for Australian television, such as Greg Matthews's James Dean impersonation when he sneered,

'Yeah, we hear you, man!' after Inspector Brown of the police force ordered him to put a sock in it; Lisa Forrest's outburst at the frustrations of having to look after Ian's foul-mouthed father day-in, day-out; and the crowning moment, Bob's forgiving Ian for his terrible crimes against him. It was magic. I'm a shy person by nature, but it was pretty easy to go out and give Roy and HG my best because they're very relaxed . . . and the fact they really wanted me to play the part was also a great comfort. I read where Roy Slaven was quoted in the paper as saying I was the man they had in mind for the role of Ian from day one: 'Sirro was the only one in the world who could play Ian.' He is vulnerable, yet strong. He is very fit and very strong and with a bit of a grin—he exudes sex from start to finish.'

As for Greg Matthews, whose character Col was portrayed much later in the series as a latent homosexual, Roy said, 'Greg adds something special to Col, a character representing the sense of Australian maledom that is unrequited—the mad lover in each of us that rarely gets a chance.'

Thousands of people have strained their brains for hours on end to work out the formula that has made Roy and HG so successful. Obviously, they're very bloody funny and what they do is what Aussies do best—they tell quality bullshit. From what I've noticed, however, they live by the old comic's creed that the best impromptu is the end result of hours of preparation. The boys and their staff spend hours pouring over all sorts of newspapers and magazines looking for scraps of information that can help them lampoon a sport or a star. Also, in one of his rare interviews as John Doyle in the Melbourne *Age*, Roy Slaven gave a few other insights into what has made he and HG such a successful commodity.

You see, John Doyle isn't your traditional sports devotee . . . as a kid he was into science, so that says a lot. However, both he and his buddy tapped into the fanaticism Australians have for sport and by behaving in the way they do behind the microphone—making it such a life-or-death matter—they're actually laughing at the people who religiously tune into them. They're probably laughing their heads off at we sportsmen too, but I love 'em too much to take any offence.

I also consider them as a great team. Neither tries to get one-upmanship over the other. Instead, they do what a lot of the great football sides do and they create safety nets so if one struggles, the other helps them out. They're two champions, and I last heard they were in London flogging beer for a big Aussie brewery. I pity the Poms because after needing nearly a quarter of a century to recover from Barry Crocker's alter-ego Bazza McKenzie, along comes Roy and HG. Take the tip—London will never be the same.

The Very Thoughts of Roy and HG . . .

Roy on football being a passionate game: 'Oh, it is passionate, yes. It's not played with the mind, it's played with the *heart*. Football takes us back to a more *rootsy* idea of people where you don't think, you just let the body perform. It's driven by instinct and intuition. Passion can be a frightening thing. You've got to be very careful with passion. It can be a fire, and you've got to be careful not to *burn*! I don't think we can deny football is a metaphor for sex.'

Roy on contact sports: 'It gives a number of people the opportunity to do things in public that they would be arrested for if they weren't doing it surrounded by a white line and a lot of people watching.'

HG on how our Asian neighbours perceive Aussies based on the way we play footy: 'Asian neighbours? We're tough, we're hard, we use the nut, we're coming, we take no prisoners, we go in hard and early, we go the squirrel grip, we don't muck about, we're coming, we're no-nonsense types.

'We're a bit thin on some of the cultural aspects but, on the other hand, there's plenty of drive from the back row. There's plenty of guts, courage and commitment.'

Roy on living at Balmain: 'I'm within walking distance of Leichhardt Oval, the Dawn Fraser Pool and Singo's tennis courts. I sometimes stand opposite Balmain Leagues Club on a Saturday night and sniff the ambience of defeat coming through the door . . .'

HG on sporting stars trying their hand at show biz: 'We've got Brian Walsh [Andrew Ettingshausen's manager] saying ET's going to Hollywood and Dermott Brereton popping up on E-Street! Well, I want to know when it is going the other way. I want to see Mel Gibson turn out for the Bulldogs for a game.

'I know he's small, but surely the boys could throw him a few easy passes.'

Roy on whether Brad Fittler should captain the 1995 Australian World Cup side: 'No, he's a very ordinary player. I know the press, especially those associated with the ARL, are trying to beat him up as the $5 million man but he's done very little, he's very flaky in defence, his attack is very ordinary, he doesn't think, he's not terribly convincing off the paddock when he's trying to handle media commitments with *The Footy Show*.'

HG on a bit of biffo in Parliament House: 'I think we are going back into a more hands-on phase, and I'd like to think Tim Fischer has the guts to come out swinging and lead us back to the halcyon days when we weren't afraid of planting one on each other in the quest for truth.

'Mick Young, in his day, didn't mind planting one on Andrew Peacock. Soon as they saw each other Mick would flatten him.'

Roy on whether they'd call a Super League final: 'I hope there are three or four Rugby League competitions next year, you know, I love the Metropolitan Cup and I hope we'll be calling the Metropolitan Cup final because I think that one will galvanise the most interest. Wouldn't it be good to see Newtown against Wentworthville in a Metropolitan Cup?'

The boys on magic Melbourne Cup moments:
HG: 'In 1974 a very enthusiastic crowd removed Prime Minister Gough Whitlam's pants and presented them to the winning jockey, "Handbrake" Harry White, who had just booted Think Big clear in the shadows of the post ...

'Harry, always short of a good pair of trousers, donned the PM's trousers and cut a very attractive figure at the Cup Ball that night. Later Harry had the daks made into four three-piece suits—one of which survives to this very day.'
ROY: 'The 1962 event is not only memorable because of Even Stevens' brilliant win but it was the year opposition leader Arthur Calwell and a former Miss Australia were found in the hay at the back of Even Stevens' float. The fruity and compromising photos taken by "The Long Feller"—jockey Jack Thompson—were

confiscated by sympathetic *Age* journalists drawn to the yellow float by the ruckus and shocked squeals of delight.'

Roy on relationships with the fairer sex: 'Something I have discovered over the years is that it's very hard to make a relationship work when you're married to sport. Sure, there's a lot of excitement at the beginning, when your partner is happy to go to pie nights, fundraising functions, or whatever. But after a while when you ask a woman to wait in the car while you go and play a bit of sport, wait in the car while you do a bit of coaching, wait in the car while you talk to Newk about the Woodies, she gets sick of waiting.'

Roy on retired players missing the headlines: 'There are a lot of players who don't get the spotlight any more, who'd like to sit in the back of a car and drive around and wave.

'I saw Chook Raper the other day and he was walking around town. A bloke bumped into him and just said, "Out of the way".

'I wondered if that bloke knew he'd bumped into Chook Raper. Poor old Chook, he didn't know him. He was a piece of history, a legend, and he was being treated like just an ordinary bloke.'

THE FORM GUIDE

CHAPTER 15

Aussies like to punt. Where else in the world do poker machines provide the main financial support for clubs? Where else is a champion racehorse stuffed and placed on display in a museum? In what other country do some jockeys enjoy even greater respect than scientists or doctors?

Like everyone else, I don't mind the occasional flutter on the nags, the pokies, Club Keno and even blackjack. It isn't that I *need* to have a bet, I just like to have a go at taking on chance . . . it adds a bit of spice to things. And I have no doubt most people punt on FootyTab for the simple reason it makes a weekend's round of football so much more interesting. Indeed, in 1996 punters outlayed almost $17 million on Rugby League with the TAB and it is at the stage now where diehard Balmain fans sweat on the results of such games as Souths—Gold Coast with an almost religious fervour.

The Rugby League ranks are crammed with gamblers and hustlers and if I had to form a dream team based on a bloke's passion for having a bet, I'd need to wade through an impressive list of names including Peter Sterling, Craig Coleman, Allan Langer, Craig Field and Terry Hill—though I'd have to give Alf Langer the captaincy. After all, the little bloke was one of the Broncos who were ordered by their coach Wayne Bennett to stay out of the TAB on a Saturday morning. Bennett adopted a hardline approach to his team's punting habits because the Broncos were losing too many Saturday games and he feared they were thinking more about their horses' form than their own.

As for my gambling on the footy I don't mind the occasional mystery bet on FootyTab, but in the wake of the infamous footy betting scandal that followed the 1994 allegations that Souths threw their game against Wests, I reckon any footballer would be a mug to lay a wager with a bookie. It is far too risky—if an upset did occur it would lead to further innuendo.

If I was a punter, however, I'd be quite particular about who I put my hard-earned cash on. I'd fight the temptation to bet with my heart because I think the TAB is definitely one place that has no room for sentiment. You have to go for the team you honestly believe is going to win, and to do that it is important to look at all the angles, such as the team's form, the available players, their strengths and weaknesses, their record at the ground where they're playing, the opposition, the weather conditions, who's injured, who . . . cripes, when I put it in that perspective it sounds like too much hard yakka for me. I reckon I'll just stick to the old mystery bet and pray to one day enjoy the same luck as those blokes who won a motza—$2 million—by placing one lousy dollar on a mystery bet. In the meantime I've put together a bit of a form guide that includes players from both the ARL and Super League just to help the punters out when they're stuck.

The ARL Stable

Brad 'Freddie' Fittler (Penrith, Sydney City): Brad comes across as a character from the teenage cult movie *Bill and Ted's Bogus Adventure*. He can be vague, and he's into video games and alternative music. However, behind Freddie's carefree facade lies a serious footballer. I'll spill the beans here and reveal he's a closet trainer who works up a sweat in the gym while his mates are snoozing. If you should ever hear Brad talk about Rugby League you'll be genuinely impressed, because he's a tremendous student with clear insights into the game. In terms of his status I rate him in the top six, behind the likes of Canberra stars Brad Clyde, Laurie Daley and Ricky Stuart.

Dale 'Rowdy' Shearer (Manly, Brisbane, Gold Coast, South Queensland, Sydney City): This guy isn't shy in coming forward because he gives the Queensland Origin selectors 'reminder' calls on the eve of an Origin campaign. In an era where the game is so deadly serious, Dale Shearer has (for better or worse) remained himself. He's still one of the best gee-up artists in the business and sometimes it's hard to gauge where you stand with Rowdy because it's difficult to tell when he's being serious or not. Yeah, he's a real enigma and I've seen him do some unbelievable things, like the time he was in the Test team and we were going through our attacking drills. When the pigskin reached Rowdy's wing it bounced over the sideline because no-one was home. Instead, Shearer was down the other end of the field kicking a ball about on his lonesome! What's even funnier is despite the fact he's only played a handful of games in the past few years, he has no trouble getting a start with a host of clubs.

Geoff 'Tooves' Toovey (Manly): He's developed into one of the game's toughest half-backs because he isn't scared to bleed. Some of the game's hard-heads, such as Mark Geyer, Tony Butterfield and Mark Carroll, rate this pint-sized No. 7 as League's most competitive player. I wouldn't dare argue—he's been bashing giants twice his size for the past decade. He's an angry ant who not only sledges the opposition but is forever on the referee's back demanding everything from a manicure to a penalty!

Cliff 'Napper' Lyons (Norths, Manly): Like a certain brand of scotch Cliffy is still going strong. While old age is fast moving in to crash tackle him, he still has the ability to bamboozle the field with his deft ball skills. He also has the uncanny ability to sniff out a try when the pressure is on, and that makes him a constant threat. As an opponent it is suicidal to allow him any breathing space.

Mark 'Spud' Carroll (Penrith, Souths, Manly): If the Spud was a racehorse he'd be named Mr Ed, because just like the nag from the old TV show he likes a chat—especially about himself! I'd love to be Don King and arrange a bout between Spud Carroll and some of his enemies, such as Newcastle's Paul Harragon and Canberra's David Furner, because they'd be the fights of the century. Nevertheless, I rate Spud highly among the game's most courageous ball-runners and would prefer to play alongside him than against him any day.

Steve 'Beaver' Menzies (Manly): The Beaver boy is sometimes mistaken by mothers and little old ladies for a member of the Vienna Boys' Choir because he's one of the most polite sportsmen you could ever hope to meet. Indeed, I'm sure I saw him help an old age pensioner cross Pittwater Road. Undoubtedly one of the most breath-taking sights in the modern game is that of Menzies charging onto a Cliff Lyons pass and sprinting through a gap in the opposition's defensive line. His main problem is most opponents are now awake to that ploy, and they stick to him like Tarzan's Grip!

Dave 'Cement' Gillespie (Canterbury, Wests, Manly): We roomed together on the 1990 Kangaroo tour and the big bushie from Narromine in central NSW ranks as one of my best footballing mates. He may be getting a bit long in the tooth now, but Cement still has the ability to hammer a ball carrier with one of those bonerattlers which once had him dubbed 'the king of crunch' by the Sydney media. His biggest enemy at the moment is calories and kilojoules because he is carrying around a bit of a belly and backside. Nevertheless, the extra weight doesn't stop him from producing the goods when the whips are cracking.

Terry 'Tezza' Hill (Souths, Easts, Wests, Manly): He can talk, talk and talk until it gets to the point where he's almost as unbearable as Chinese water torture! He's a good player, and apart from being very strong Terry's also deceptive because he's much quicker than he looks. His wingers should patch up any differences they may have with him because he doesn't seem keen on giving them the ball. I rate him, especially in the wet, since he's used to running with the spray from his lisp . . . er, lithp!

Paul 'the Chief' Harragon (Newcastle): As Phillip Street's highest paid player, the Chief has a lot of added pressure to perform these days. While I regard him a class act he is vulnerable to making a mistake, such as conceding a penalty at the wrong time in a game. Nevertheless, punters are correct to consider the boy from the northern NSW coalfields as an extremely intense competitor. I've long believed his motto is to take no prisoners.

Anthony 'Butts' Butterfield (Penrith, Newcastle): Another tough old nag still doing the rounds. Butts thrives on knocking the bigger names down with his trademark kamikaze tackles. He doesn't let friendships stand in the way of playing tough football either, because in their first encounter against one another Butts smashed Mark Geyer's nose, and they were childhood friends. Butts has paid for his fearlessness with some frightful injuries, which have hindered his career. If he could last an entire season Butterfield would be up there with the likes of Tallis, Geyer and Co. as one of the most feared men in the game.

Marc 'MG' Glanville (St George, Newcastle): After twelve years in first grade it appears as though MG's appreciated by everyone except the representative selectors. Glanville ranks highly in my books as a skilful back-rower who has always led by example. Apart from a high workrate I regard him as a hard, but fair, competitor. At the beginning of the '97 season MG appeared to be one of those top players destined not to represent his state or country. And that stinks.

Paul 'Mary' McGregor (Illawarra): This hard-running centre didn't crack grade football until he was a mature twenty-three, but he's definitely made up for lost time by establishing himself as a fully-fledged international. He's loved by the Wollongong crowd, but Lady Luck has been a bitch and kicked him in the nuts a few times and his career has been hampered by injuries that would test anyone's patience.

Rod 'Wishy' Wishart (Illawarra): Blond-haired, blue-eyed and bloody crazy, Wishy is a rock-solid winger who hails from Gerringong on the NSW south Coast, home to yet another thoroughbred named Mick Cronin. Wishart has an army of fans thanks to his ability to fill in as an extra forward. Indeed, he's so effective he could hold down an extra job as a police horse to break up riots! He's also saved the day for Australia and Illawarra on numerous occasions with his reliable goal-kicking.

Paul Langmack (Canterbury, Wests): Langmack talks up a great storm in the dressing room, on the paddock, off the field and probably even in his sleep. He's driven plenty of players—including some of his team-mates—around the twist with his constant chatter, but Lord knows he's been a solid and consistent performer from the back row for a bloody long time.

The Super League Stable

Laurie 'Lozza' Daley (Canberra): After spending his formative years in grade as a rebellious tearaway who thought bedtime was when the bar closed, the Raiders five-eighth has developed into not only a champion competitor but the consummate professional. His efforts to keep Canberra in the running for a grand final berth in 1996 while the Raiders' other superstars were injured was worthy of a medal. Laurie is one of the most loved blokes in the game because he has never placed himself above the people who idolise him. Football-wise he's worthy of being regarded as perhaps the world's best player.

Bradley 'Clydie' Clyde (Canberra): Clyde by name, Clydesdale by nature. Clyde ranks alongside Laurie Daley as perhaps the world's greatest player and I think testimony of his ability is the fact some rivals reckon the best way to stop Brad is to whack him around the melon when he has the ball. The Raiders back rower is great on any track, and he can be depended upon to never let his team-mates down. He's an unassuming champion and considered a great role model.

David 'Furnsie' Furner (Canberra): A tough kid with plenty of ticker, Furnsie and I share an empathy because we were both dropped from the Australian team after the shock first Test loss at Wembley on the '94 Kangaroo tour and we consoled one another by getting smashed. He's a likable bloke and I definitely consider him a man's man—no-one jerks him around.

Brett 'Mullo' Mullins (Canberra): A lean, mean flying machine who is capable of length-of-the-field tries from fullback. Mullo is blessed with enormous potential, but we won't ever see the best of him until he harnesses his well-publicised nocturnal habits. Perhaps he already has . . . but I'm adamant, when this kid is on fire he's white hot.

Andrew 'ET' Ettingshausen (Cronulla): Here is a genuine thoroughbred who improves with age. Even though he's now in the 'boiler' class, ET is still considered by star-gazers as one of the game's great pin-up boys. Actually, I'd go as far as to nominate Andrew as the ideal role model for any kid because he's a guy who does all the right things. He doesn't smoke or drink to excess, he's extremely well mannered and he hasn't allowed himself to get caught up in all the hype. Another plus in his favour is he's never tried to protect his model good looks. He certainly throws himself into the thick of the action to the extent that I regard him as one of the game's toughest competitors.

Les 'Bundy' Davidson (Souths, Cronulla): A slow-talking, good-natured country boy who produces his best in tough conditions. He's considered by some people as the game's best bar-room brawler, yet, as is the way with the really tough guys, I haven't seen Les throw too many punches. He's a good bloke who stands tall in the modern era because he has retained the old-fashioned values, such as never letting your mates down.

Allan 'Alf' Langer (Brisbane): This cheeky but lovable little bloke from Ipswich is always good for a belly laugh away from the action. His make-believe wrestling matches with Kevin Walters are unbelievable to watch because you'd swear they were fair dinkum. On the paddock, however, there are few more serious competitors. Langer is a shrewd, scheming half-back who has made himself a punter's favourite because of his passion for mixing it with the bigger boys.

Steve 'Pearl' Renouf (Brisbane): One of the great natural talents who has speed, acceleration and a smart football brain. There are few players who can turn a game with a step and lightning run like Renouf. Like all the great artists, however, he does need some pushing and sometimes even a rocket to get him moving.

Glenn 'Lazzo' Lazarus (Canberra, Brisbane): I've seen this fellow develop from a roly-poly reserve for the NSW Primary Schools team twenty-long years ago to become one of the most effective front-rowers in the business. Lazarus has tremendous ability to make hard yards and to get up quickly to play the ball. While that helps give his team a roll over the opposition, I don't necessarily agree that trait alone makes him the best prop in the world. I reckon there are a few more skilful and athletic props than my roomie from the 1994 'Roo tour, but it's the same old story . . . I'd much rather play alongside him than against him.

Wendell Sailor (Brisbane): If this fellow was a racehorse he'd turn a positive swab for caffeine because he's the original Coca-cola kid. This blue ribbon athlete even drank the stuff before breakfast on the 1994 Kangaroo tour. Apart from a definite sweet-tooth, Wendell has the ability to be a great player. His value to the Broncos has risen because not only can he match muscle in the forward pack but he's capable of streaking away for a try in Carl Lewis fashion.

Michael Hancock (Brisbane): He should be called the pinball wizard—not because he can play the pinnies, but because he bounces off opponents like a maverick pinball. Micky may come across as an angry young man because of his aggressiveness. He kicks and bucks and pushes and cusses during a game, but take it from me, Mick is one of the most personable blokes you could hope to meet away from the game.

Gorden Tallis (St George, Brisbane): With his explosive running style Tallis has the potential to be remembered as one of the game's most devastating forwards of all time. He has spent a few seasons fine-tuning his temperament, but I think Gorden may have now realised he doesn't need to live up to other people's expectations of how tough he should be.

Robbie 'The Moth' McCormack (Newcastle, Hunter Mariners): Here's an honest toiler from the bush who is tough enough and good enough to star alongside the elite players. When the state selectors picked him for the NSW Origin side a few years back, he fitted straight into the big time. He's an inspirational player and before he agreed to play with News Ltd's Hunter Mariners, he was regarded as the heart and soul of the Knights.

Steve 'Boxhead' Walters (Canberra, North Queensland): Yet another street-smart hooker who puts everything on the line. Steve is capable of making yards from tractor-like runs from dummy-half and I'd have him on my side any day—well, providing Benny Elias wasn't available. Nevertheless, he's a player you can depend on to pull a trick or two out of his magic box when the pressure is on. Away from the action he and his brothers Kevin and Kerrod are Rugby League's answer to the Three Stooges, though I'm not sure which one is Curly.

Ian 'Iron' Roberts (Souths, Manly, North Queensland): Ian is a genuine warrior. I don't think he's played a game fully fit in the last decade, and I reckon it's amazing to think that back in 1990 *Rugby League Week* was asking whether Roberts could survive the rough and tumble of top grade football because of his high injury rate. Well, he has. No matter what you may think of his decision to declare himself a homosexual, I reckon it would take a tough marker not to admire the fact he puts the good of his team ahead of his own health. Ian has often made himself a target in the past by playing in some of the big games on one leg.

Mark 'MG' Geyer (Penrith, Balmain, Perth): If this big fella is given half a chance he'll run his own race, and he'll offer no apologies for it either. Mark needs a coach who is prepared to work with him. As much as I like him as a friend, I hope he knows time is fast running out for him to make the most of his obvious potential, which has been suppressed over the years by hefty suspensions, rifts with clubs and personalities, a regrettable positive drug-test and his other personal problems. In terms of good guys, I'd nominate this self-confessed Rugby League rebel as one of the most generous blokes I've come across. If the bullets were whistling overhead and the enemy was about to launch a bayonet charge, I'd definitely want MG beside me in the trenches.

Greg 'Brandy' Alexander (Penrith, Auckland): A star indeed, but I reckon Brandy sometimes needs to wear blinkers and not be distracted by what is going on around him. Although Greg is yet another competitor in the dreaded veteran class, he still has the skill and brains to be a threat on the right track. He's rejoined the Panthers after a few years in the wilderness and I'm certain his nouse and love for his home district will rub off on many of the young kids out at Pantherville.

Phil Blake (Manly, Souths, Norths, St George, Canberra, Auckland): Phil's in the same bracket as Greg Alexander, a classy half-back–five-eighth or fullback who is now compensating for his loss of speed with intelligence. He is one of the most travelled competitors in the game and he's always added that extra 'something special' to whatever team he's aligned himself with.

At Pasture ...

Steve 'Blocker' Roach (Balmain): He always played at top weight, but Blocker was still one of the classiest players I've ever seen. His ball skills were unparalleled by any forward of his era and when it came to the power of intimidation this genuine front-row legend had his opposition walking on eggshells. However, there were occasions when he'd cause his team-mates to tear their hair out in frustration because he'd concede a stupid penalty—such as whacking an opponent on the whiskers within goal-kicking range of our posts. Nevertheless, the big fella certainly made life interesting for all those around him.

Wayne 'Junior' Pearce (Balmain): One of Australian sport's great champions, Junior deserves to be remembered as the man who revolutionised Rugby League. He made himself a guinea pig by dining on alfalfa sprouts and mung beans at a time when the average footballer's lunch was still a meat pie and a schooner. The Tigers lock changed that line of thinking by learning all he could about vitamins and carbohydrates and their role in improving a footballer's performance. His results were so impressive it didn't take too long for every fair dinkum player to embrace parts of Junior's New Age advice. As a skipper I don't think too many blokes could rally a side quite like Junior because he always led by example. He'd throw himself into the opposition's defensive line with such frequency there were times when I feared he was going to seriously hurt himself. Nevertheless, no-one is perfect and if I had to pick a fault, for want of a better word, it would be he wasn't a naturally skilful player. However, Wayne got much better results because he worked much harder and more determinedly than most other players.

Benny BE Elias (Balmain): Another street-smart hooker who could get under the opposition's guard, and skin, with a cunning dummy pass or swift sidestep. He suffered many setbacks throughout his time, such as losing the captaincy of Balmain and NSW when his career was in full swing. Nevertheless, he had many fans and one of the greatest accolades he received came from the 1948 Kangaroo team's hooker Frank Johnson, who said he couldn't recall a hooker who had the complete skills of 'Balmain' Benny. He was a great drawcard, in the sense that Lebanese-born Cahiben (Ben) Elias attracted fans from a different background to the game. He wasn't scared to make it known that he didn't get on with some of his rival hookers, and his blood feuds with Mario Fenech and then Steve Walters were unbelievable.

Garry 'Jimmy' Jack (Wests, Balmain): Jimmy was one of the game's safest fullbacks and if ever you needed to depend on the last line of defence he was the man because few opponents got past his cattle dog-like defence. And when it came to defusing a high bomb, he was unbelievable. He was a real professional—it didn't matter if he was playing in front of 40 000 at the Sydney Football Stadium or 40 for Salford in England, he'd give his utmost. When I think of Jimmy Jack I recall a player who was as tough as a mule . . . and one who had the head to match!

Mick 'Ginger Meggs' Neil (Wests, Balmain): A spitting image for the comic strip character Ginger Meggs, and just as cheeky with the ball in his hands. This skinny, red-headed kid gave Balmain plenty of thrust from five-eighth and like Junior Pearce the key to his secret was the fact he boasted a tremendous fitness level. His heart was so big I'd have backed him to run five Melbourne Cup races on the one day!

Gary 'Wiz' Freeman (Balmain, Easts, Penrith): This cocky little Kiwi loved to upset his opponents with a mosquito bite of a punch or a rough face massage. He was a scheming half-back with such a strong will to win he'd do *anything* he could to rile his opponents. I'll never forget the fact he tried to ruffle my feathers in a Test match with a few slaps across the cheeks—the ones on my face!

'Slammin' Sam Backo (Canberra, Brisbane): Slammin' Sammy was no show pony, and as for looks, well, I'm being kind when I say he'd never challenge Mel Gibson or Brad Pitt for the title of the world's sexiest bloke. However, Hollywood Mel wouldn't hold a candle to him as an international front-rower because Sam was one of the most explosive forwards from a short run-off. If he was 5 metres out from the opposition's tryline and charging at full speed, it needed a good man to stop him from crashing over the line.

Wally 'The King' Lewis (Brisbane, Gold Coast): A definite one-off who could dictate a game by slowing it down to a long yawn or speed it up to a breakneck pace. Wally's skills were always destined to have him sit alongside the game's masters, but in my mind he elevated himself to great heights because he could do such things as manipulate the referees in ways no other player has yet managed—though Manly's Geoff Toovey is doing his best to try and better him. To anyone who may not have ever seen Wally play my advice is to believe all you read. I already know that one day in the future I'll be telling my grandkids that I played alongside him—he was *that* good!

Mal 'Chicken George' Meninga (Canberra): Mal will be long remembered from Canberra to Cumbria as the people's champion. To reach the lofty heights of Australia's Test skipper he overcame such adversities as racism and four broken arms. And once he made it to the top he definitely didn't let anyone down. Off the field Chicken George was a great ambassador for Australia—and on it, he was close to unstoppable. He's never backed away from any challenge and it will be interesting to see how he goes coaching Canberra from 1997.

Terry 'Baa' Lamb (Wests, Canterbury): A durable little fellow whose depth of courage was best summed up by his rallying Canterbury to a memorable 1995 grand final win over red-hot favourites, Manly. Baa had been unable to train with the 'Dogs for most of the season because of crippling knee injuries, but you'd have never known it by the way he played ... it was something special. He'll also be remembered as the man who put his personal life before footy when in 1982 he sacrificed a berth on the Kangaroo tour to remain in Australia and marry his fiancee, Kim. It spoke volumes about the cheeky little bloke's priorities.

Gene 'Geno' Miles (Brisbane): Blessed with speed, size, strength and stamina, Gene established himself as one of the game's royal centres throughout the 1980s. Along with Mal Meninga and Wally Lewis, he was one of the foundations Queensland built upon to dominate the State of Origin series for too long a bloody time. Once Miles finished his career in Australia he crossed the Atlantic and conquered Britain as a member of the champion Wigan side.

Paul 'Fatty' Vautin (Manly, Easts): He's done for transvestites on
The Footy Show what Elle McPherson has done for swimwear. Even
in a sequin dress Fatty is a genuine legend, and if you don't believe
me ask him yourself. I hope his new career as a television celebrity
doesn't diminish from his proud playing career, because Fatty was
capable of turning a game with a clever pass or quick burst from
the back row. I thought he was a good and consistent player, but
he left the punters wondering what the heck he ate for breakfast
whenever he pulled on a Maroon jumper—then he played at an
even higher level.

'Bustling' Bob Lindner (Parramatta, Gold Coast, Wests, Illawarra):
A genuine Rugby League aristocrat who was often accused by his
detractors of giving his all in representative matches and not backing
up in the week-to-week grind of the premiership. I copped the same
barbs … It's funny how we players see things very differently from
the so-called critics because my memory of Bob Lindner was of a
class act. I loved playing alongside him for Australia because he was
as safe as a two dollar coin in Jimmy Jack's wallet.

*Trevor 'the Axe' Gillmeister (Easts, Brisbane, Penrith, South
Queensland)*: Anyone who was ever sized up and smashed by a
Trevor Gillmeister 'special' realised he was tougher and harder than
the average bear. For many years he slogged away, battling for
greater recognition, and unfortunately he didn't get it until towards
the end of his career. I always had a deep sense of respect for this
crash-tackler and believe me I'm being sincere when I say I don't
miss this Queensland tough nut's big hits at all.

BEST OF THE BEST

CHAPTER 16

When I had trouble picking my *Best Ever* team a good mate suggested I put myself in the selectors' shoes and copy them. When I asked him what that meant, he suggested I whack on a tight-fitting green blazer, order a huge Chinese feed, glean as many opinions on certain players as humanly possible, read the headlines to see who is getting the most positive publicity ... and then stick to the same team that was picked the previous season. There's no need to point out my mate is a bit of a cynic. Picking my personal Best Ever team has rammed home just how tough a job the selectors have. I don't envy their lot—no matter how good a side they pick, it is impossible to keep everyone—like my buddy—happy. Someone is always going to be overlooked, and when I finished selecting my team I was embarrassed to see such names as Ricky Stuart, Steve and Kevin Walters, Greg Alexander, Paul Harragon, John Cartwright, Ian Roberts, Bobby Lindner, Brett Kenny, Sammy Backo, Gene Miles and Gary Freeman were left on my shortlist. I was embarrassed because they rank among the modern game's greatest players.

Playing selector has been an interesting exercise. Apart from learning about *their* frustrations, it has also reinforced how lucky I have been to graduate from being a snotty-nosed East Ryde kid with dreams of playing for Australia to actually brushing shoulders with some of the game's greatest stars. I don't like to think too far down the track, but I'm certain that appreciation will only grow stronger in the years to come. Actually, I pity poor little Curtis and his brother: they'll have heard plenty of 'war' stories from their old man by the time they're old enough to vote.

Now, after squeezing into an old national blazer and feeding my face with dim sims and sweet and sour pork I've picked my side, and no matter what some critics may think, I'll stand by it for better or worse.

Fullback

Garry Jack: I don't think any footballer who knows Garry has forgotten to give him a 'pay' about his protective qualities when it comes to looking after his money—and I, for one, have no intentions of sparing him.

Benny Elias swears Garry holds onto his cash so tightly the Aborigine on the two dollar coin winces. I, however, witnessed Jimmy's generous streak the day a woman from the *Save the Dolphins* fund knocked on his door and asked for a donation. Without a moment's hesitation the Balmain great ran out to his laundry and returned with a huge bucket of water and told the girl, 'Here, build the bastards a house!'

Gary Belcher, the former Queensland fullback who roomed with Jimmy on the '86 Kangaroo tour, loves to recall the time he rolled back into their room at about 3 am on the morning of the third Test. On tour most players put their coins in a glass or an ashtray on the dressing table between the beds and don't really worry about it unless they need to buy a newspaper or a block of chocolate. As Belch tiptoed across the room in a valiant attempt not to disturb Jimmy's slumber, he just about crapped his dacks when Jimmy suddenly rolled over and boomed in his foghorn voice, 'Badge, I'm missing three quid from my glass. Did you take it?' That was so much like my mate Jimmy—despite the fact he had an international to play he spent the entire night tossing and turning because he was determined to get to the bottom of the missing money.

Even that incident paled in comparison to the time when Garry won our Big Spender award at Balmain's annual awards night. The awards are just a bit of fun; we gave the NRMA award to the club's worse driver; the casanova award goes to the fellow with the greatest libido; and there's the club drunk trophy. Anyway, as Jimmy stood on centre stage to accept the Big Spender award all the boys started throwing coins at him and you wouldn't believe it, while he offered his words of thanks he kept bending down to collect the coins.

I've seen some great fullbacks since I was a kid, and for a time I adopted Manly's Graeme Eadie as my favourite player. However, I don't think any No. 1 has played with the fearlessness of Garry Jack. He'd do crazy things like charge into the biggest and hardest player on the opposition's side. If it came to last-ditch defence I was always confident when Jimmy was on deck because I knew if anyone managed to break through our line he wouldn't only pull 'em down, but he'd smash 'em.

Whenever I'm asked about Garry Jack the player, I recall the time he lost a few teeth when we played North Sydney. Rather than leave the field for treatment Jimmy simply bent down and put them in the front of his socks, and got on with business. And, no, I wouldn't dare suggest he put the teeth in a glass that night to see if the tooth fairy would leave him any coins . . .

Winger

Andrew Ettingshausen: My first memory of Andrew was when we were both seventeen and members of the Combined Catholic College team that competed in the 1982 Australian Schoolboys selection trials at Newcastle. ET made a big impression on all the guys when we pulled in at McDonald's for a meal break and the girls behind the counter drooled over him. It was bloody sickening! After a few minutes we other blokes grew restless because the service came to a grinding halt as the silly sheilas ogled this long-haired kid with the surfie looks. To his credit ET didn't lord it over us, he simply laughed at the attention—and he still does.

One of the most amazing aspects about the rise and rise of Andrew Ettingshausen is he hasn't allowed any of the fame or many trappings of his success to affect him. He's a guy who has beautiful girls swoon at his feet, yet he looks straight past them. Instead, Andrew is a happily married family man who'd much rather prefer a night home watching videos with his wife and kids than raising hell in a nightclub. I consider ET a pretty good mate and while we've known each other since the McDonald's incident of '82, we

121

spent plenty of time together on the '94 Kangaroo tour when our wives shared a house on the outskirts of Leeds, along with Nicole McGregor and Gil Wishart. As a matter of fact, Lee-Anne, Monique, Gil and Nicole still meet for lunch every so often, but the time and pressures of top grade football don't allow me, ET, Paul McGregor and Rod Wishart to spend the afternoon chatting over a cappuccino. I'm certain, however, that we'll have the odd barbecues once we retire to recall some good times . . . and magic footy moments.

As for being appreciated for his football skills, I'm afraid ET has always had to compete with his pin-up boy image. For a long time some people couldn't see past his smile to what a bloody good athlete he is. And the annoying thing is, he's getting better with age. I've always respected ET's ability but he *really* made me sit up and take notice one afternoon in 1990 when he hammered me with a *huge* tackle. See, I always targeted Andrew when I ran at the Sharks line because I had my doubts about his tackling ability . . . Well, that changed in an instant as he bundled me over the sideline. I can vividly recall thinking, 'Crickey, he's worked on his defence!'

In an age where the game's powerbrokers are creating instant heroes, ET still ranks as the perfect role model for kids because his playing career has been without any major controversy. Although in saying that there was the time when a court awarded him the kind of money that would bail a Third World nation out of debt after a magazine published a balls and all shot of him under a shower while on the 1990 'Roo tour. Before the advent of Super League it was one of the most talked about incidents, but I must say after looking at the photo—yeah, just once!—I honestly couldn't see too much for Andrew to worry about.

Centres

Ellery Hanley: I don't like toilet humour, but the Black Pearl has the worst smelling flatulence I've ever had the misfortune of coming across. Our lockers are next to each other in the Tigers dressing room at Leichhardt and I should remember to buy a gasmask. The man reeks—it's putrid! Whenever I ask Ellery why on earth he can't do the right thing and drop his guts outside the dressing room he replies in the most refined English accent this side of Buckingham Palace, 'Because, Paul, it makes me chuckle.'

Stench aside, Ellery ranks alongside Wayne Pearce as one of Rugby League's consummate professionals. He doesn't drink or smoke, he eats well and trains extremely hard. When he joined Balmain in 1988 he added an extra dimension to our back line because he helped galvanise our centres, a position some rivals considered a weak link. He's also an intensely private man who doesn't relax around strangers ... but I didn't think there was any excuse for his behaviour during the 1990 Kangaroo tour when he refused to acknowledge Blocker, Jimmy and me throughout the Ashes campaign. When I saw him at the beginning of the tour he ignored my greeting of 'G'day Pearl!' by walking past me. While my being brushed annoyed me, I didn't want to think ill of Ellery so I put his behaviour down to some sort of psychological ploy. However, his stand-offishness continued after we won the war and it was pretty ordinary. I don't know, perhaps Pearl was unhappy at losing yet another Test series to the boys from Down Under.

Mal Meninga: Peter Jackson, one of the funniest buggers ever to pull on a pair of footy boots, likes to tell the story of how, during the great bushfires of '94, six fire engines were diverted to Canberra because there'd been reports of Mal's eyebrows catching on fire. Yep, he's a big man, with big eyebrows, and in the years to come I'll always remember playing alongside Mal as one of the great honours of my career. Apart from his class and skill, he is one of Rugby League's great people. He treated everyone equally and as a player I found nothing was too much to ask of him. Even as the skipper of the Kangaroos he didn't place himself on a pedestal. It was always possible for any of his team-mates to approach him and he was quite forthcoming.

One of my big regrets as one of the joeys on the '86 Kangaroo tour was I had very little to do with Wally Lewis; my shyness made it impossible for me to talk to him. I guess I feared the kind of reception I'd receive from the King because he had an aura about him. In 1990, however, Dave Gillespie and I were stationed in the room opposite 'George' and we'd often go across the hall and camp in his room to watch music videos or order ice-cream and fruit salad—at his expense. It was all good, positive stuff and I definitely got a lot out of it.

I can't add that much more to the volumes of words that have already been written about Mal's playing ability, but I'll never forget the time I played alongside him in '86 when the Kangaroos played Halifax at Thrum Hall. Mal kicked off and he followed the ball through to smash some poor Pommie bastard with the biggest tackle you could ever imagine. A hush came over the crowd the instant their hometown hero was hit by the Meninga express. Everyone feared Mal had killed the bloke! It was bloody brutal. But in my mind that one tackle best sums up Mal's power and strength.

Winger

Tim Brasher: 'Brash' by name, brash by nature, Timmy has always been a cocky bloke. I remember the afternoon in 1989 he was first pitchforked into first grade as a seventeen year old. He was on the bench at Penrith Park when Warren Ryan sent a message for our trainer to get Tim out on the paddock, and fast! Timmy got the message but he spent a few moments rooting about in his bag. Well, the poor trainer grew anxious about the delay because Warren was screaming for Brash to get a move on. The trainer refrained from pressuring Tim—he figured the kid was searching for his mouthguard. Well, as it turned out he wasn't. Brash pulled out a brush and fixed his hair before charging out to battle! None of us could believe it, least of all Wazza Ryan who, up until that moment, thought he'd seen *everything*.

When I read about Timmy being offered $700 000 to join Penrith last year I couldn't help but chuckle at my memory of when he joined the Tigers as a schoolboy, because the little bugger never had any money. During the semi-finals in '89 we'd go swimming every Thursday night and then, as part of our preparation, the entire team would have a meal at a restaurant. We gorged ourselves for $25 a head. Well, that kind of cash was beyond Timmy's reach back then so we'd all chip in to buy the young fella a feed. I laugh at that memory nowadays because Tim could buy the joint out if he wanted to. I made Brash see red last year when the newspapers broke the news of his deal with Penrith, because it coincided with our match against Norths in which he missed some telling tackles. They definitely didn't help our cause and after the game I said, 'Brash, you've been offered $690 000 for your attack and $10 000 for your defence.' And boy, it went down badly. Despite my tongue-in-cheek barb, I rate Tim as one of the game's elite players. Apart from his explosiveness he can also play fullback, wing, centre or five-eighth.

Five-eighth

Wally Lewis: On the 1986 Kangaroo tour of Great Britain and France I felt as though Wally was the King and I was the big, clumsy court jester, and I found it very hard to approach him. It isn't as if he did anything to make me feel that way, it was just something I felt as a result of my being young, shy and awkward. Which is a pity, because I've spoken to Wally since he retired and have found him to be a very interesting and accommodating bloke. Instead, I admired his skills quietly and from afar. They were awesome. Wally could do *anything* with the ball, and he also possessed a brilliant kicking game, a tremendous running game and an amazing power to intimidate referees. I don't know if there has been anyone who could read a game quite like the King; he could see a hole forming in the opposition's defensive line two tackles before it was there. As someone who played against him in the Origin I have no hesitation in nominating Wally as one of the masters of the game. One thing I found quite interesting about the man is he not only played a few kilos above his weight throughout his career but he also never objected to a cigarette or a can of beer!

Half-back

Allan Langer: A few champion half-backs, such as Greg Alexander, Peter Sterling and Gary Freeman, have crossed my path in the past but this little bloke from Ipswich stands out as the cheekiest of 'em all. He creates numerous headaches on the paddock because he's such a smart player . . . and in more ways than one. I remember in one Origin match at Lang Park hearing a familiar voice call, 'Go left, Sirro!' as I prepared to run the ball up, and like a mug I followed the order. Well, you can imagine how much of a boofhead I felt when I realised it was Alf, the little bastard, who had yelled out at me as he ran back onside.

But that's Alf. He's a laugh a minute and you can count on him to break the tension of a tough match by warning a hulking prop, 'Watch out or I'll give it to you, mate!' I could never help myself when I heard him say that and I'd always break into a huge smile. I also found it was a laugh a minute when I heard Allan recall some Ipswich tales with his childhood pals Kevin and Steve Walters on the '94 Kangaroo tour. You could make a soap opera about what went on in their small Queensland town. Yet the funniest image I could conjure from hearing them carry on was that of Alf, dressed in his blue singlet, stubbie shorts and working as a truckie for the council. It's almost as bizarre as picturing Sharon Stone running in a race at Wentworth Park.

As I've already stressed Alf is a smart player, and even at thirty-something he still has the brains, if not the speed, to make him a handful for his opponents. Since his Lang Park gee-up I've always made it a point to see who makes any call before I run the ball up!

Prop

Glenn Lazarus: I shared a room with Lazzo on the '94 Kangaroo tour and he's a gold medallist snorer. I'd spend half the morning pulling the curtains and bed sheets out of his nostrils because he was *that* bad. Actually, it wasn't uncommon for me to leave our room on some nights to bunk elsewhere because his snoring was almost as loud as the artillery bombardment which signalled the beginning of the Battle of El Alamein in 1942. Lazzo, I pity your missus, mate.

I've seen Lazzo progress from looking like the roly-poly kid in the children's movie *Willie Wonker and the Chocolate Factory* when we played in the NSW Primary School team, to being a super-fit back-rower with a Sergeant Slaughter haircut for Canberra, and then becoming Brisbane's answer to the Michelin Man because of the extra padding around his hips, belly and butt. However, Glenn has always been going in the right direction—forward.

He's been valuable for the Broncos because he's able to speed up a game with his quick playing of the ball and his ability to run the ball up straight and hard, and while I admire those attributes I don't believe Glenn matches Blocker for sheer skill. He learned the value of nutrition from Steve when they roomed together on the '90 'Roo tour . . . they stored more sweets and chocolates in their bar fridge than a Darrell Lea chocolate shop, but Blocker insisted they drink diet cola because it had only one calorie. They were unbelievable, and I reckon the kids in Northern England were glad to see the back of the Aussie Test props because they bought so much confectionery to see themselves through the tour that Manchester and Leeds were forced to ration their chocolate. I even heard one old dear tell her grand-daughter, 'This is what it was like during the Blitz, love,' as they waited in line for their chocky!

Hooker

Benny Elias: Just before the 1997 season kicked off I saw Benny on Channel Nine's *Sale of the Century* quiz show. It was a celebrity game and he was at his competitive best against the singer Jon English and actress Amanda Muggleton. Anyway, Benny mispronounced an answer and the host, Glenn Ridge, passed it on to the judge. When the judge ruled Benny had stuffed up, the Tiger terrier turned around and denied he said what he said. Man, that was Benny all over. He was one of the most super-competitive players I ever came across, and I don't know how he developed that edge but he'd become an overnight millionaire if he could bottle it. The amazing thing about Benny was if he saw an opportunity, he'd go for it even if it went against our pattern of play and even though that caused our coach Warren Ryan plenty of grief, Benny stuck to doing what he did best.

I believe what made Benny's success in Rugby League even more spectacular is if you judged him on his size—or lack of it— he should never have played first grade. He was only 170 centimetres (5 feet 7 inches) tall and a slight 71 kilos (11 stone 3 pounds) when he made his first grade debut back in 1982. He was big enough of a Rugby League identity, however, to be regularly caught in drama and controversy That might have put him offside with some fans, players and administrators, but I reckon Benny thrived on it.

He had his fair share of enemies, and mate, they weren't just your usual onfield duels—they were dead-set blood feuds. President of the 'I hate Benny' club was former Souths and Norths hooker Mario Fenech, and North Queensland's Steve Walters and former Newton and Canterbury rake, Mark Bugden, vied for Mario's position. The amazing thing is while Benny would bait Mario with some terrible sledges, he confessed he was terrified of what would happen if Fenech just snapped and lost the plot.

Perhaps the greatest show of support I could ever have offered Benny came in 1992 when Alan Jones stripped him of the captaincy and gave me the job. I knew Benny was hurting, and while I now consider the club's captaincy a great honour it didn't mean as much to me back then as it did to Ben . . . it didn't feel right about having the little 'c' next to my name in the *Big League* program and knowing how much it upset Benny. I spoke to Alan about giving him back the job and I'm glad Jonesy followed through my request.

Prop

Steve Roach: As you can tell by his efforts on *The Footy Show*, Blocker is a very funny bloke and, take it from me, he's no overnight sensation. The big fella has spent years perfecting his craft by geeing up people, and in my rookie years I was a regular fall guy for many of his jokes. Actually, his send-ups have given me a great insight into his character. I can now reveal without any fear of contradiction that he's just a big kid at heart.

I was given my earliest glimpse of Blocker's sense of humour on the eve of my first grade debut against Parramatta in 1986 when he cornered me at training to say he'd bumped into the tough Eels forward Paul Mares at a promotion at the Merrylands RSL earlier that day. Roachy said he had a message from Maresy, and the gist of it was Maresy planned to rip my head off and kick it into the mob on the hill. The message riled me and by match day I was all pumped up to steamroll Mares or any other would-be assassin. Anyway, before the kick-off, for some reason Blocker kept pointing my way with a smirk on his dial . . . and that's when the penny dropped—the bludger had been geeing me up all along. He tried it a few more times before he realised I was aware of his tactic.

I don't think there have been too many greater shows of strength on the footy field than Steve Roach charging into the opposition's defensive line with his knees and elbows pumping hard and high. Purists will long remember Blocker as a classic front-rower because he was tough and hard and he enjoyed bullying the opposition. I was one player who benefited from his reign of terror because I estimate I scored 75 per cent of my tries courtesy of a short Blocker pass after he'd sucked the defence in. While they were like gifts from heaven, Steve was definitely no angel. There were times when he'd concede silly penalties, and they were hair-tearing-out material. I guess the fact he had the opposition walking on eggshells because they feared him helped balance the ledger. And the way he'd rev the opposition up, like former hothead Mario 'Test Match' Fenech, was unbelievable. He'd snarl such things as, 'Call yourself Test match? You've gotta be f. . .in' kiddin', mate' as he packed down for a scrum, and it would have the right impact. Mario's eyes would start rolling and his getting square with Blocker would become the focus of his game.

Second-rowers

Mark Geyer: This nomination may surprise a few people but I have no hesitation in naming the volcano in my team. I remember the time he ranked among the game's most destructive back-rowers. He was tough, and I'll never forget the afternoon in 1989 when he took it upon himself to try to tame the Tigers pack after his Panthers team-mate John Cartwright was sent off. It had been a spiteful game, MG went ballistic—he took a swing at Benny when he alleged my little mate had chomped him on the finger. But after Geyer finished lodging his onfield complaint, he was sinbinned for ten-minutes and there was steam coming out of his ears as he trudged off the field. On his return MG targeted *me* and he ran at me for the rest of the game with all the power of a runaway train. It was a challenge I welcomed, and while Balmain eventually won the game 33–6 I'm certain anyone who witnessed Geyer's effort that afternoon would remember the tenacity of it.

MG has a reputation as a hothead, but I wouldn't be surprised to learn one day that a lot of it was a bit of a front, like the night on the '90 Kangaroo tour when he suddenly snapped against Halifax. He was whacked in a tackle and when our trainer Brian 'Sheriff' Hollis ran out to revive him with the magic sponge he started screaming, 'I'M GOING TO KILL SOMEONE!' ... *'I'M GOING TO KILL SOMEONE!'* Well, Sheriff had no idea of what to do and he seemed to look towards Bozo on the Aussie bench for an answer, but he realised all was well when the big bloke tugged at his sleeve and whispered, 'I'm only joking, mate.' Sometimes I wonder how many other times the big bloke has given a wink and dismissed a trademark 'tantrum' as nothing more than a gee-up.

There is nothing staged about his ability, however, because on his day MG boasts some of the best ball skills you could ever hope to see from a forward. He can throw a great cut-out pass, he can challenge the line and he sure does know how to cream an opponent. I think the fact he and Mark Carroll were nicknamed 'Crash' and 'Bash' in England because of the way they tried to bowl over the Pommies with big shoulder charges, gives you an insight as to where he comes from in the defensive department. Sadly, Mark has allowed too many off-field problems to affect his form and one of my deep regrets is unless he gets it all together—and soon—I fear MG will hang his boots up knowing he didn't fulfil his potential. He'll be remembered all right, but it seems as though it will be for all the wrong things, such as his dramatic exits from Penrith and Balmain, his testing positive to a drug test, his chest-to-chest battle with Wally Lewis in the 1991 Origin and his all-too-frequent visits to the judiciary. When he played for us at Balmain in 1994 I could see glimpses of the old magic and, as I've already said, I hope my mate can turn it all around.

Bradley Clyde: When Clydie made his debut against Balmain in 1988 he was so badly mauled by the Tigers he trudged off Leichhardt Oval wondering whether he was good enough to play top grade football. The poor bugger was only eighteen and he'd been targeted for some extra attention by us. I read where he even compared our search-and-destroy mission to a turkey shoot. When a few of us spoke about that 'Clyde-kid' after the game, however, we all agreed he was a champion in the making. He was strong, fit, athletic and courageous, and he had star written all over him. Clydie has exceeded everyone's expectations by establishing himself as one of the modern game's best players.

His worst enemy over the years has been injuries. Clydie has been laid low by such shockers as having his ligaments pulled away from his shoulder, needing a shoulder reconstruction, suffering anterior and posterior cruciate damage in his knee, and he lost most of last year when he was ruled out of action by an ankle injury. I have no doubt the high injury toll is a result of his tremendous workrate, because Brad plays like a man who sets goals for himself in every match he plays. He's the first man to follow *every* kick through, he seems to be the bloke who takes the first hit-up and he's always in the thick of the defensive action. His enthusiasm has worried a few people over the years including Canberra coach Tim Sheens, who feared Clydie risked burning himself out. Sheens ordered him to cut down on his workrate, but Brad still finished matches with forty-odd tackles and twenty-something hit-ups. Actually, I almost choked on my Cornflakes after Canberra's slow start to the '97 season when I read in the newspaper Clydie faced a move to prop! I could understand where Brad was coming from when he told *Rugby League Week* he wouldn't appreciate playing there when he thought he still had something to offer as a back-rower. I couldn't agree more, and I reckon playing Clydie up front at this stage of his career would be akin to using Phar Lap as a plough horse.

Clydie's philosophy on Rugby League is the team with the most hunger and desire normally wins the premiership points, and that's exactly how he plays. When I think of Brad Clyde the man, I think of the old adage, 'You can take the boy out of the country, but you can't take the country out of the boy.' He's very laid-back, and after getting to know him in the various representative teams I doubt that he'll die of a heart attack, because he's so relaxed. All in all, Brad's a great bloke and he was always someone I was happy to have pack down alongside me.

Lock

Wayne Pearce: I've played alongside—and against—some of the world's greatest players but none has ever matched Wayne Pearce for sheer determination. I'm not being disrespectful when I say this, but Junior should never have played for Australia. He wasn't a natural like Wally Lewis or Mal Meninga; instead, he made it to the top because he worked much harder than anyone else. In the heat of battle he often shamed me and the bigger blokes at Balmain because even though he was 3-stone lighter than us, he'd be the first to grit his teeth and run the ball into the opposition's line or pull off a big hit. Blocker would sometimes say, 'C'mon mate, the poor bastard will kill himself if we don't do something!' And he was right.

Wayne was also a bloody good team man and I remember the day we played Parramatta at the WACA in Perth in the mid-1980s and I found myself in trouble as two heavyweight Eels forwards ganged up on me and started swinging punches. I've long maintained that even though I was screaming for 'help' I had the situation well under control, but Junior didn't see it that way. He whacked on the Superman outfit and came to my rescue by landing a punch on one of my attackers . . . Poor Pearcy finished the skirmish with a broken thumb and I think he missed eight weeks as a result of it. Sorry, Wayne.

It's well known Junior pioneered diet and nutrition for foot-ballers—he used to rattle like a bottle of vitamins, he scoffed that many—but the amazing thing about his strict standards, which included no grog, smokes or junk food, is that he didn't ever stray from them. Well, except for the night I saw him rip into a bucket of hot chips. I felt guilty for him ... but I'd seen him stick to the straight and narrow far too long to 'chip' him! And he had plenty of chances to stray, such as the day we beat Cronulla in '88 and became the first Balmain side since the 'legends of '69' to make it through to the grand final. The mob went berserk, and while you could have got drunk on the atmosphere—(and a few of us did)—Junior refused to buckle to numerous requests to have a swig of champagne.

One of my big regrets as a Balmain player is I wasn't at Leichhardt when Wayne played his last game. I was over in New Zealand with the Australian team, and I'm being fair dinkum when I say I thought about him before we played the Kiwis. Indeed, whenever I'm asked what Wayne Pearce was like as a player my immediate response has been 'A champion', and I guess it always will be.

Reserves

14 *Laurie Daley:* Choosing my five-eighth between Laurie and Wally Lewis was easily my toughest selection, and the King only got home on the flip of a coin. It must be great for spectators to see Lozza play, because whenever he struts his stuff they're watching a man who loves his job. He plays with such passion. I was one of many people who were surprised when he didn't win the 1996 Rothmans Medal since he single-handedly held the Raiders together when Ricky Stuart, Brad Clyde, Brett Mullins and all the other Canberra stars succumbed to injury. Like Wally, Laurie is a freak. He reads the game well and can dictate the tempo by running the ball or throwing pinpoint-accurate passes. I especially admire his compet-itiveness, however, because Laurie is one of those blokes who'll keep trying no matter how the scoreboard reads. And win or lose, Laurie is the first to shake hands with the opposition. He also has real leadership qualities, but I think the great thing about Laurie's success is it has come after he tamed a wild streak which saw him live his life like a vampire—of a night he partied in the pubs and clubs around Canberra and slept most of the daylight hours away. His skills were always undeniable and I, for one, am glad he didn't allow them to come a distant second to his inclination to party.

I enjoyed weight training on the 1986 Kangaroo tour. John Leatherbarrow

Fe Fi Fo Fum, I love running through the Englishmen. Andrew Varley

A few of the boys would have paid me good money if I whacked prankster and occasional trainer Brian Hollis on the '94 tour.

With George Treweek, considered by many judges as the games finest second-rower, before I left with the 1986 Kangaroos

Big Jack Gibson pondering the
meaning of life at his home

Sirro and Lee-Anne with son, Curtis

The happy class clown, centre stage, middle row   Sironen Family

Despite his superstar status, Laurie is another player who hasn't allowed success to go to his head. Fans have found him to be very approachable. He's had everyone from homeless people to high profile politicians throw their arms around him and he's treated them all with the same sense of respect. One of the sad aspects about the Super League war was the fact guys like Lozza, Mal, and to a lesser degree, Clydie, took a bucketing from some sections of the public when they stood up for what they believed in. Despite our being at different ends of the game's new political spectrum, I have no trouble in nominating him as one of the best blokes I've been associated with through football.

15 *Peter Sterling:* Sterlo was never afraid to back himself on the field, and he lived by the same creed off it. I've never known a bloke who could gamble the way he did. On the '86 Kangaroo tour he amazed me by not seeming to care if he lost a few hundred pounds on a game of blackjack. It was a big eye-opener but it also summed up the bloke's carefree spirit.

At his peak, the call from any team who opposed Parramatta would be to shut Sterlo down. That was easier said than done, however, because Sterlo was a bit like Roadrunner, who made poor old Coyote look like a real drop kick. As a matter of fact, I can clearly remember feeling like a goose during my rookie year when I took it upon myself to rough up Sterlo in a tackle. He got up and shaped up to me and as I half-smiled at the sight of Sterlo being reduced to an angry ant, I felt like a big bully and I let him be.

The man who discovered Sterling in 1977, former Parramatta coach Terry Fearnley, believes Sterlo's destiny in Rugby League was preordained. When Fearnley travelled to Wagga to sign him, he felt as though the blond kid's path had already been mapped out. Sterlo won almost every award the game had to offer, including the Rothmans Medal, the Dally M Medal, the Clive Churchill Medal and the NSWRL's Writers Award for the best player in 1986—and he won some of them several times. These days he should be in contention for one of the Australian entertainment industry's most prestigious prizes, the Mo Award, because he's brilliant on *The Footy Show*. And as testimony to his standing in the game Peter can do all the stuff Fatty, Blocker and the boys are now famous for, such as dressing up in drag or playing a limpwrist, and still have enough credibility to make important observations about the game.

16 *Terry Lamb:* Considered to be one of the game's great characters who knew how to mix a bit of fun with the serious stuff, in terms of his playing strengths Terry wasn't unlike Timmy Brasher in his versatility. Indeed, it was Baa's versatility that allowed him the unique honour of playing in *every* one of the '86 Kangaroo team's tour matches. He was given his chance to play first grade with the battling Wests Magpies, and he went on to become one of Canterbury's greatest ever clubmen. He played a record 349 first grade games. He was a great leader and anyone who played alongside him at Belmore would agree he was a great source of inspiration. Indeed, even today Terry runs the water bottle for the Canterbury Super League team and I'd have to think long and hard before I could think of any player with a junior football competition named in their honour who'd do such a menial task.

Baa was a funny little bugger, and I'm sure all the members of the '86 Kangaroo will long laugh about the day we were treated to a rather boring tour of a castle in Carcassone. We were being shown chandeliers and old paintings of poofy-looking Frogs from four hundred years ago and were bored out of our skulls. It started to get interesting when we heard a ghostly-sounding voice coming from an ancient trunk begging, 'HHHeeellllppppp meeeeeeee! HHHeeellllppppp meeeeeeee!' I think our guide just about wet his pants when the lid on the trunk creaked open and Terry sprang out screaming, 'Gotcha, ya bastards!' Not to be outdone, Paul Langmack and I climbed up the belltower and while Langers started swinging on the rope, I stuffed a pillow down the back of my shirt and pretended to be Quasimodo, the Hunchback of Notre Dame. It was a great lark and I think Aussies have been barred from the castle ever since—not that they're missing anything.

I share the same sentiments as Simon Gillies, Canterbury's 1996–97 skipper, in thinking it was a pity Terry didn't play his last game as a five-eighth in a premiership-winning team. Instead, he played hooker in a side that didn't go all that well. I'd have loved for him to bow out a winner after he spearheaded the Bulldogs to a gutsy win over Manly in the 1995 grand final, but I guess it doesn't matter in the grand scheme of things.

17 *David Gillespie:* When Cement Gillespie lost half a finger in an industrial accident which cost him a berth on the 1986 Kangaroo tour, I'm told he used the deformity to his advantage over the

summer. Legend has it whenever Dave went to a bar he'd simply hold his hand up to order four schooners and a middy! He's a lot like that, Cement—he's retained his no-nonsense bushie streak despite cracking it in the Big Smoke.

Dave is one of my best mates in the game, and I love catching up with him whenever time allows because it's always a big drink with loud laughs. There were times, however, when I did my best to avoid him like the plague, like in the mid-1980s when he was regarded as the 'King of Crunch' because of his stinging defence. But I like to call Cement the 'Sprinkler' because I find whenever we go out for a drink on the bourbon he's always leaving to water himself . . .

18 *Brad Fittler:* Freddie is a freak. When he was presented with the 1995 World Cup trophy by Prince Andrew at Wembley Stadium there were no airs or graces—the boy from Penrith simply said, 'How ya' doin' dude?' before grabbing the silverware. But that's Brad Fittler all over—he's full of confidence, which helps him get away with such things as chatting up the Christmas tree in the lobby of the Holiday Inn at Leeds during the 1994 Kangaroo tour, and telling the audience when he was named *Cleo* magazine's 1997 Sporting Bachelor of the Year that he was 'in touch with his inner-personality'.

Freddie's confidence—and talent—has been there for all to see ever since he burst onto the scene with Penrith as a seventeen-year-old schoolboy. He was a knockabout kid back then, but he now has the image, profile and respect traditionally reserved for the sport's superstars. He may not have appreciated that status before he was made Aussie Test skipper, but Brad was made well aware of the responsibilities which go with his profile soon after his comment on live television that the best thing about being in camp with the Origin team was getting 'pissed with the boys'. It went down like a lead balloon with the Phillip Street heavies and they demanded he get his act together. He's certainly a lot more polished these days, but I reckon deep down Freddie is still a Huckleberry Finn-type who'd much rather be locked in a room playing computer games or out with his mates instead of doing lunch with the high-powered corporate types he's obliged to meet through his position in the game.

When Brad toured with the Kangaroos in 1990 he adopted the approach that he was there for a good time, if not a long time. He went to town and packed on plenty of beef after overdosing on the Pommie beer and the greasy North English junk food. He was renamed 'Fat Freddy' and his penance was to work the unwanted lard off in the 'Fat Boys' club'—a Bob Fulton initiative for the boys who appreciated the good life a little too much.

There are many people who believe Fittler really came of age when he skippered the so-called 'Best of the Rest' Australian team against a red-hot Kiwi side in 1995, and I won't disagree. It was the first time in years that Australia had started a Test series as underdogs, but I don't think anyone banked on Fittler's class and skill. He helped steady the green and gold ship and he inspired the boys to blow the Kiwis out of the water and win the series 3–0. Anyone who saw Freddie pot his field goal from 42 metres out will long remember it, because it seemed as though Brad had challenged himself to see if he could do it. Well, he landed it and after the match, coach Fulton hailed him as the world's greatest player. While it was a great wrap I reckon we're still to see bigger and better things from Freddie Fittler.

THE CLIPBOARD BRIGADE

CHAPTER 17

I plan to take up coaching when I finally drop anchor and settle on the north coast of New South Wales, and while I anticipate a peaceful lifestyle on the beach, I expect coaching will cost me what's left of my hair. I know that because I've seen how the stresses involved with the job have affected the likes of Frank Stanton, Warren Ryan, Alan Jones and even Junior—and believe me, it isn't pretty.

During my thirteen years in grade I've formed my own theories on what makes a good coach. I think the guys who really make it are the ones who have a quiet self-confidence. They don't need to constantly throw their authority in your face because they know the players respect them, and they definitely don't try to impress outsiders. The really good coaches also talk to their players rather than jumping to conclusions about what they may have heard second hand and, naturally enough, they know their trade.

I reckon the clipboard brigade lead a tough life. No matter how good a coach may be, he lives and dies by how well his players execute his ideas. It must be rough for a lot of them to sit in the grandstand and watch their team go through the motions. Indeed, the great Wally Lewis gave an insight into that frustration when he said of his time at the helm for the Gold Coast and even the Queensland Origin side that, 'Being a coach, after spending all your life before that as a player, the big thing is sitting there watching your team play and not being able to do anything . . .'

When I was in Hawaii learning how to play gridiron I read the philosophies of many top American Football coaches, and I reckon a bloke named Bear Bryant best addressed the way a coach makes it all click when he said, 'I'm just a plough hand from Arkansas, but I have learned how to hold a team together. How to lift some men up, how to calm down others, until finally they got one heartbeat together, a team. There are just three things I'd ever say: 1, if anything goes bad—I did it; 2, if anything goes semi-good, then we did it; 3, if anything goes real good, then you did it. That's all it takes to get people to win games for you.'

In the modern game the coach commands plenty of media attention, and it is a common sight after a match to see a crowd of journalists hang off their every word. Indeed, I think the veteran radio commentator Frank Hyde said the scene was akin to watching Moses deliver his sermon from the mountain. The coach is grilled on everything from who he considered his best player to who finished the game injured. I'm certain it must be hard for a coach to let go of a bad result and start all over again. We players at least have the luxury of a few days to regroup our thoughts, but they have to go 'cold turkey' and get on with it.

A coach lives and dies by his decisions and I reckon one of the hardest things about being in charge of a first grade side would be the fact *everything* about the job is so public. His triumphs and tragedies are very visible. Actually, the great American novelist James Michener, a Pulitzer Prize winner, best summed up the unforgiving glare a coach can find himself living under when he wrote, 'If he is of a sensitive or retiring type he has no place in coaching. If he is deficient a crowded stadium witnesses his failure, and he is not allowed to remain deficient very long.'

I've learned my trade from listening to the coaches who have guided me with the Balmain, NSW and Australian teams since 1984. Unlike Laurie Daley, however, who plans to coach first grade one day, I haven't kept notes on individual coaches and their methods. Instead, I believe the little things go a long way. I don't reckon the relationship between a player and his coach can be underestimated because it definitely has a bearing on a player's outlook. I know of some instances where teams have lacked troops of genuine first grade standard but they were competitive because of a fierce will to win for the coach. I know myself, when I think of how good a coach was I base it on such things as if he showed an interest in me; whether he showed faith in me; and if he really knew what was going on. They were the blokes I'd bust a gut for when the chips were down.

It will be interesting to see how I survive if I do coach in the bush league one day. I've been blessed with an insight into the job by playing under some of the best in the business, but I admire the form of Johnny Cochrane who coached the Sunderland soccer team in England 60-odd-years-ago. Apparently the job of a coach back then was to simply assemble a good team and leave them alone to play soccer, and Cochrane's only role on match day was to stick his head around the dressing room door moments before a game—while puffing on a cigar and swigging on a flask of whisky—to ask the team, 'Who are we playing today?' The team would reply, 'Arsenal, boss', and with that he'd laugh, 'Oh well, piss on that lot', before staggering back to his seat in the grandstand. We players at Balmain may have driven some of our coaches to levels of despair, but I'm glad to say our bosses were much more professional than old Johnny Cochrane. My memories of them on an individual basis are as follows:

Peter 'Duff' Duffy (1984–85): There haven't been too many people to match Peter's devotion to duty as Balmain's reserve grade coach. He loves the Tigers so much I reckon Duff still bleeds black and gold whenever he nicks himself shaving. Peter may have been the perennial reserve grade coach, but I don't think there could have been a better bloke to help guide the Tiger cubs through their initiation to grade footy because he was a no-nonsense type and he refused to accept anything but a player's best.

I remember him as a strict disciplinarian who valued performance and effort above reputations and excuses. In other words, he'd blast anyone who didn't put in. Peter hasn't changed since I first met him fifteen years ago and he still has the kind of poker face you see on the barmen in those old wild west movies just before the good guy and baddie shoot it out. As for smiles, well, I'm afraid even in retirement they're still as rare as Haley's Comet.

Peter had the right attitude for a reserve grade coach and he accepted his priority was to ensure first grade fielded its best possible. To achieve that objective Duff had to spend time helping out-of-form 'stars' get back on track, and he also had to ensure his own players could be relied upon to play first grade at any given time. It probably wasn't the best edict for a coach to operate under since it lessened his chance of winning the reserve grade premiership title—but Peter placed the good of the club ahead of his own aspirations.

Peter demanded good ruck plays, variety and tap moves, and he was all for keeping the game pretty simple. And he was like that even away from the game, because Peter 'Balmain' Duffy can be very blunt.

Frank 'Biscuits' Stanton (1986): Wayne Pearce delights in telling the story of when he turned up to Leichhardt Oval early one afternoon and saw Frank Stanton place a saucer of milk outside my locker. When Junior asked what the hell he was doing, Frank cursed, 'Well, the bastard is playing like a cat!' That was Frank all over— he was a prickly old coot who could make you feel like a schoolkid with one of his stern looks. And I credit Stanton's strict discipline and standards as one of the reasons Balmain emerged as a premiership force in the mid to late 1980s.

He was the kind of man we needed to give us the right direction and in retrospect I reckon his philosophy that to spare the rod you'll spoil the child was exactly right for a few of us. Frank, who coached Manly to the 1976 and '78 premiership titles, taught us that top grade football was a serious business . . . and he was likely to do anything to reinforce it. For instance, I read about when he took the 1982 Kangaroos on a bus ride ten miles into the green English countryside. Some of the boys figured they were going on a sightseeing tour before training, but that notion was shattered when the bus stopped in the middle of nowhere and he barked, 'Now run back to the hotel!' Yep, that was our Frank all over.

Frank didn't crack a smile all that often, but he realised he wasn't paid to impersonate Luna Park . . . he was in charge of a group of footballers who, by nature, look for weaknesses in their coach's character. I'll long remember how in my rookie year Frank would regularly take me aside and urge me to get more involved in the game. I lacked confidence back then and I thought I didn't have the right to override my seniors, such as Steve Roach and Wayne Pearce. Because Frank was always on my back, however,

I progressed from being a reserve grader to a Kangaroo in one season.

Billy Anderson (1987): Technically, Bill Anderson is one of the smartest football brains in the business, and he's a lovely guy to boot. He was wonderful at explaining moves and what he wanted from us in a clear and concise manner . . . but, and there is a but, under Billy our intensity, and dare I say our discipline, dropped off because he lacked the same sense of authority as Frank Stanton. We still played good football nevertheless, and after eleven rounds we led Manly on the premiership table by 3 points . . . but our entire campaign fell apart when the Sea Eagles thumped us 48–14 at Brookvale. We fell into a hole that was too deep to climb out of. Sometimes I wonder what the scenario may have been in '87 had it been Stanton or Warren Ryan demanding we re-focus after that setback. All this isn't intended as a slight on Bill. Indeed, it was Bill Anderson who made me take a long, hard look at myself the afternoon he told David Brooks and me that we were too nice to be first grade forwards. Bill said we played like blokes who could lose their space in a car park to a queue jumper and cop it sweet, and when I thought about what he said I realised Bill was spot on. I lacked the natural meanness of, say, a Gorden Tallis and I worked harder on trying to establish my authority.

Unfortunately I didn't play my best football under Billy. I returned from the Kangaroo tour carrying a few extra kilos and a groin injury that gave me curry. As the season progressed my form was atrocious, and Bill did the right thing and dropped me to reserve grade to help me get my act together. These days he works as Wayne Pearce's right-hand man, and his contribution to the Tigers' revival has been outstanding. As I've already said, there are few better tacticians than Bill Anderson and I value his opinion.

Warren 'Wok' Ryan (1988–90): Poor old Wok has been caught in more personality clashes with his star players than a prima donna on the set of a TV soap opera. He had his faults but I loved being coached by him because he brought out my very best. Everything Ryan did at Balmain was deadly efficient—there was a purpose to *everything*. Whenever I spoke to Warren the thing that riveted me were his eyes . . . they seemed to burn straight through me as if he was looking for something that no-one else had looked for.

Lord knows Wok's eyes were blazing the day he arrived at Leichhardt and took me aside for a chat. Warren spelled out what people expected from me. Because I was a big bloke, he said the mob wanted to see me make the line-breaking runs and big tackles, and as it turned out, he was a part of the mob. Warren was a godsend for me after the horrors of '87 and as we spoke I felt a genuine confidence when he assured me it wouldn't take too long to rediscover my true form.

He helped me find it by instilling a meanness throughout the entire Balmain camp with what he called 'Wazzaball'. You won't find a definition of it in any dictionary, but any footballer who observed it will tell you it was a ruthless, fast-moving defensive game rounded off with clever blindside taps, clinically efficient kicks and a quick exploitation of the opposition's errors. Wazzaball led to low scorelines and accusations that it killed off attacking football, but it worked. With Ryan as our guide we unleashed a brutal brand of defence on the premiership and along with guys such as Junior, Bruce McGurie and David Brooks I enjoyed being a part of the game's toughest defensive unit. There was an air of confidence and ruthlessness at Leichhardt because we believed no-one was good enough to get the better of us.

Warren reinforced that feeling in his words. For instance, whenever he pushed us hard at training he would say, 'The deposit is in the bank now, we'll make the withdrawal on Sunday.' Sure, it was corny, but we believed it . . . we wanted to believe it. And our training session didn't just end after a shower—we'd have regular team meetings at a local restaurant and the table would become a strategy board as Warren used salt and pepper shakers and cutlery to emphasise how he wanted to see us execute a move.

He wasn't much for individual razzle-dazzle and I guess he didn't believe in having one bloke shining out in what is a team effort. After Warren finished telling me he expected to see me mix it some more, he told Benny to knock the *puste malaka* (Greek for wanking) out of his dummy-half play! He could be like that, the old Wok; he didn't worry about reputations. If Warren didn't believe a player could serve a purpose to the team he'd let everyone know. For instance, I'll never forget the controversy that followed his declaration that Ross Conlon was the worst player ever selected to represent Australia in 1984. That statement raised quite a few eyebrows because 'Roscoe' was playing under him at Canterbury.

Some people considered Warren a little too arrogant for his own good, but I didn't find that. My memories of Warren Ryan are of a man who not only helped me get back on track but the coach who gave the Tigers two shots at the grand final.

Alan Jones (1990–93): Alan Jones was as much out of place as coach of Balmain as a bottle of chilled Chardonnay at a pub frequented by wharfies or bikies. His appointment as Balmain's coach made headlines because his only experience as a footy coach was with the Australian *Rugby Union* side. I'm afraid to admit it, but Alan had little concept of what Rugby League was about. Indeed, when he arrived at training with the edict that 'the man with the ball was boss', we pretty much kissed goodbye all the years' worth of work we'd invested in developing structured play under Ryan, Stanton and Anderson.

There were times when I shook my head at his concepts because they had no place in Rugby League. Yet, as we tried to absorb his 'new' ideas aimed at revolutionising the game Alan would stand before us at the team meeting and implore such things as, 'Run at space not face!' It was almost like being in his radio studio as he read the slogan for a commercial.

I can't dispute that Jones tried, and tried hard, to help many of the young kids in the club, but the fact is most of them were so far out of kilter with Jonesy's world his analogies were lost on them. He'd call some things the 'Gucci factor' because he maintained the quality remained long after the price had been paid. But to some of the young battlers who'd grown up in Housing Commission estates in Glebe and Annandale or on properties in the outback he may as well have spoken Latin—and, come to think of it, he sometimes did.

Some of those same kids exploited his caring nature by getting out of training because they pulled up sore from their last hit-out. It angered me and plenty of the other players to see them sit out a session because we knew how Peter Duffy, Warren Ryan, Frank Stanton and Billy Anderson would have reacted to a player whinging about a bit of soreness—with absolute contempt. I even chipped a few of them about their slack attitude, but it was to no avail because the bloke with the clipboard had the final say.

Unfortunately, such incidents eroded the senior blokes' respect for Alan. I can well recall the day we were sitting about in a circle as he gave a pep talk at training and Benny started pulling faces behind his back. Well, I started sniggering which caused a chain reaction and the other guys broke up. When it became a straight out symphony of laughter Jonesy lost it and he shouted at different blokes, 'What are you laughing at, you're one person who shouldn't be laughing!' It was like being in a classroom, and I still consider it a sad state of affairs that the side had degenerated to such an extent.

Alan did a lot of good things for Balmain, such as luring sponsorship dollars to the club and taking a genuine interest in most of his players, but blokes such as Jimmy Jack and Gary Freeman couldn't believe what was happening at Leichhardt and they vented their spleen to the press when they left the Tigers. They made caustic comments accusing Jones of possessing a limited knowledge of the game and cultivating an inner circle of favoured players. As the team skipper I tried to douse the flames by defending Alan in the press, but I'm afraid by that time things were too far gone to save us.

Despite his many problems at Balmain I still consider Alan Jones a great achiever. After all, his breakfast radio show on 2UE constantly rewrites the ratings record books; he has the ear to some of Australia's most powerful people; he's a former tennis champion; he attended Oxford University; and he helped the Wallabies come of age on the international Rugby arena. And as the man who penned speeches for former prime minister Malcolm Fraser he could perhaps steal a line from the most famous of them to sum up his stint at Leichhardt. You know the one; 'Life wasn't meant to be easy.'

Wayne Pearce (1994–97): Wayne and I are good mates but by the end of his first season as our coach I was ready to bale out of Balmain because I didn't want to stick around and see the stress of the job change his positive outlook on life. Wayne and I had been through too much as players and friends for me to allow that, and I told him how I felt.

I was dead-set ready to leave, but when I spoke to Junior I saw a bloke who was expected to work miracles that weren't possible. He had a few players who weren't putting in, and as a competitor who threw everything into his game, Wayne couldn't cop it. He considered Balmain as an army that didn't want to fight a war and it outraged him. Actually, he went ballistic . . . everyone was made to pay for the bad elements' sins.

As we were hammered from pillar to post in Wayne's debut season as coach, his pain was clear for all to see. Indeed, he wasn't much fun to be around for a while, and nor was Balmain. He rectified that at the end of the year, however, by wielding the axe and cutting thirty-eight players. He replaced them with young kids from the bush and from the lower grades of other clubs who wanted a chance. And he took their energy and their hunger and he instilled a fighting spirit into them.

His decision paid off because in 1996 the Tigers finished just one game short of achieving a modern-day fairytale—a semi-final berth. While the Tigers missed the cut we dented some mighty reputations, such as Newcastle, Canterbury and Auckland. It was great and even though Junior had pushed me up to the front row I felt invigorated—it was a throwback to the old days.

We had kids such as Glenn Morrison, Mark Stimson, Mark O'Neil and Darren Senter pick up from where Blocker, Benny, Brooksy, Buckets, Jimmy and Meggsy had left off . . . And it wasn't just on the paddock, because Junior helped foster a great camaraderie by organising team dinners and functions that involved our partners. He rebuilt the Balmain I knew and loved and in the process Junior was back to the bloke I'd always known. He's now in charge of a side that overflows with creativity and enthusiasm, and he's enjoying himself. Actually, my greatest wish for 1997 is the Tigers will do well for Junior because the bloke deserves it.

Don Furner (1986 Kangaroos): Don Furner would have to rank as perhaps the most affable man to ever carry a clipboard. I believe it was Don's easygoing nature that helped blend the New South Wales and Queensland players into a crack unit on the '86 Kangaroo tour of Great Britain and France at a time when State of Origin passions were at their fiercest. The year before Don was given the national coaching job the Australian team was divided into two camps after a bitter Origin series and accusations that the New South Wales and Australian coach Terry Fearnley had displayed a bias against the Queenslanders during the 1985 tour of New Zealand.

Interstate rivalries notwithstanding, Don was in charge of an Australian team that was of such a high standard the Kangaroos only had to do such things as play touch football at training and they'd still whip the opposition. Don's Aussie-bush logic made tour life interesting. For instance, on the day we played Halifax at Thrum Hall he insisted we run uphill in the first half so we'd have the downhill run when we grew tired in the second half!

When Don retired as the Australian coach he became a selector, and I'm grateful to him because he certainly showed plenty of faith in me over the years.

Jack Gibson (NSW, 1989–90): He's regarded by his army of admirers as the 'master coach' and his achievements in the game stretch a mile long. Jack has ensured his place in Rugby League's book of history by introducing such innovations to the game as having his players listen to motivational music before games; being the first Sydney coach to use a computer to store records and file each player's data; analysing films; making regular trips to the United States to link up with American Football franchises to learn anything that was applicable to Rugby League; and, in 1967, he was the first coach to order his troops not to retaliate to rough-house tactics.

Guys such as Peter Sterling are real Gibson apostles and they talk about Jack with a sense of a reverence. At the risk of sacrilege, however, I'm afraid to admit that when he coached the NSW side in 1989—unbelievably his first major representative side—it was all a bit of a mystery to me because the man spoke in riddles. As far as I was concerned there was no rhyme or reason to our plan and it was hard to know what was expected of us. I remember asking my second row partner and skipper Gavin Miller whether I'd defend as the left or right defender and he summed up the confusion of the team when he said we'd defend wherever the ball was. Well, as it turned out, we were all over the place in the first match and we were donkey-licked 36–6. It was my first taste of Origin football and I didn't know what hit us . . . and as the Queenslanders hammered us for eighty minutes I thought to myself, 'Get me out of here!' It was tough, and apart from me the game also represented a baptism of fire for Mario Fenech, Brad Clyde, Laurie Daley, Chris Johns and John Cartwright with Greg Alexander on the bench for the first time. Gibson told the press there was no point in sticking with the same side, which had been defeated, the following year. He figured if we were going to be done over again it may as well have been done with some new faces.

I found it bizarre that Jack chose to ignore Steve Roach in a series where New South Wales needed some starch up front. Also, unlike Queensland, we didn't go into a team camp because Jack didn't think we needed time to meld together. In hindsight, I reckon we needed all the help we could get back in 1989.

I regret that playing under Jack wasn't the experience I'd have liked it to have been because I'm well aware of the legend. However, against Queensland we were doing what I can only call 'radical' things—we'd put up mid-field bombs and we'd constantly roll the ball forward. It was all too off-key from what the majority of us were used to.

Tim Sheens (NSW, 1991): Unfortunately, I didn't get much time with Tim when he coached the Blues because I injured my knee in the first game and it cruelled my chance to gain an insight into what made him such a successful coach at club level with Penrith and Cronulla. I do remember he came across as a decent bloke who did his utmost to bring out the best in a NSW team pitted against a very tough Queensland squad.

Bob 'Bozo' Fulton (Australia, 1989–94): I'm always going to remember Bob Fulton as a bloke who showed some faith in me when others might have opted to display caution. For instance, in 1989 he picked me to tour New Zealand with the Kangaroos after I'd been dropped by the NSW selectors. That faith meant a lot to me and I always did my best to justify it!

I've heard Bozo described by some people as one of Rugby League's ruthless characters, and I agree. He's the closest thing possible in Rugby League to a political animal. He's trodden on many toes during his lifetime in League but there can be no doubting his professionalism as a coach. Going into the 1996 grand final his win–loss ratio was 66 per cent—eclipsing the great Jack Gibson by 4 per cent.

As a coach Fulton swears the toughest thing about his profession is sitting in the stands and knowing his performance is in the hands of thirteen players. I don't think I'm shedding any new light on the bloke when I say Bozo has found ways to skirt around the rules to give his team an extra edge. For instance, he instructed his troops to exploit the head bin rule in the '87 grand final as a way to give them a break from the unusual September heat. As a player he was renowned for intimidating the referees and he's passed on a few lessons to help his players keep the whistleblowers walking on eggshells. There have been other ploys as well, such as Manly's supposed edict to (allegedly) 'nose-bomb' the opposition team's kicker. The Roosters claimed that rather than charge the ball down in general play the Sea Eagles targeted the kicker. Rather than be upset by the stinging accusations, Bozo told the Roosters to wake up to themselves.

When it comes to stirrers, Bozo is gold medal material. There aren't too many who can match Fulton's needle and some people even believe he has a real school bully streak because he does such things as nominate people for his annual Ugly Men of League Calendar—and no-one is spared. Some people say his stirring goes a bit too far, but Fulton remains unrepentant. I read about the time when a reporter asked Bozo how Manly winger John Hopoate felt about being nominated one of his Ugly Men. Bob went into overdrive saying, 'Well, he knows he deserves it . . . and take a look at your head, you're on the way too!' It was classic Bozo. There are some people who believe Fulton could be anything he put his mind to. Indeed, the widely respected League scribe Ian Heads once suggested Fulton could probably end up prime minister if he wanted, and I wouldn't disagree. Mmm, Bozo as prime minister . . . I can imagine it now. The opposition would be called 'Nevilles' (as in nobody), the Manly players wouldn't be taxed and Brookvale would probably be renamed as the nation's capital.

Phil Gould (NSW, 1992–94): I have no hesitation in nominating my stint in the NSW team under Phil Gould's direction as one of my most productive times as a representative player. Gus instilled a great desire in us to humiliate the Maroons after years of getting our butt kicked by Wally and his gang.

Phil worked hard to foster a die-for-your-mate spirit in the Blues and that certainly meant a lot to me. Indeed, by the time he finished giving one of his pep talks I felt as though I could take on the Queenslanders by myself. In others, like Brad Clyde and Paul McGregor, he worked hard on building up that spirit. While we were in camp we'd do things like go tenpin bowling, see movies, hit the grog and even sing off-key around the piano in the wee hours of the morning. We made a terrible racket, but crikey it made us feel like a real team.

And the bonding doesn't end with the last of the pre-match hangovers. Gus tells war stories before the team goes out to battle to get the adrenalin pumping. Clydie reckons the stories had such an impact on him he'd walk onto the field feeling as though he could take a bullet for his mate, and I felt the same. You see, Phil tells yarns about blokes like a US Marine who spent three years training for combat, and this guy'd constantly remind himself he owed it to his country to die in action if a war ever came. Then, when the dressing room buzzer sounds to let us know there are only two minutes until kick-off, Gould screams, 'This is it ... think about war! You're going to battle! Think of those people who have gone to war ... they blew a trumpet, they fixed their bayonets and they knew they were gunna die! Think about 'em ... now, go out and *die!*'

Talks like that would make the hairs on the back of my neck bristle, and this feeling gave us the edge that Queensland had over us for all those years. Indeed, I think Phil Gould should be regarded as the man who helped destroy the myth that the Queenslanders were superhuman at Origin time. Up until he took over as the NSW coach the Maroons had won nine out of twelve series. Under Gould we won five out of six series ... and that says it all.

UNCLE SIRRO'S ADVICE COLUMN

CHAPTER 18

Experto Credite—Believe one who knows
by experience.

Virgil (70–19 BC)

T here are no short cuts to success in a sport such as Rugby
League. It's a real man's game and a combatant earns his
stripes by proving he is made of the right stuff to back up from
some of the hardest knocks a professional athlete can expect to
take. Nevertheless, I'll always consider myself fortunate to have
been able to draw upon the experience of some real heavyweights
when I was graded with Balmain in 1985. For instance, I could
bail up Junior Pearce about diet and nutrition, Blocker was always
within backslapping range to give extra encouragement when we
faced the ferocious Canterbury or Souths packs of that era and
'Cranky' Frank Stanton was the perfect coach to mould a rookie's
outlook on the game. Frank was from the old school—he took no
crap and he demanded his players display a genuine devotion to
duty.

At the time of writing this book I'd survived the intensity (and sometimes, the insanity) of 200-odd first grade games and I've learned a few things about the rough and tumble of the game. Some of my lessons came from making errors, others were from listening to the right people, and the rest came from making observations of my own. Because I graduated through a system where the older heads passed on tips to the young rookies freely and generously, I've taken it upon myself to help out any fair dinkum young players at Balmain who ask for it. I think it is so important the older blokes nurture the young and in an age where the almighty dollar has become so important, I'd be bitterly disappointed if that ever changes. By passing on some advice we older fellas are putting something back into the game.

It's funny, you know, because nowadays when kids ask me to give them my 'best' piece of advice I don't go into the old spiel about how to break a tackle or pop a pass; my immediate inclination now old age is moving in on me is to tell them to try to enjoy every moment of their career. It's quite frightening how quickly the time flies . . . it goes way too fast. In the meantime, I hope my thoughts on some subjects which are now part and parcel of *every* footballer's life might help a few rookies to get a different perspective on various subjects. I also trust my advice will give the fans a much clearer insight into the mechanics of being involved in top grade football . . . there's much more to it than bash and barge!

Managers

Question: What's the difference between a manager and a red belly snake? Answer: You can trust a snake.

I make no apologies for sounding feisty on the subject of player-managers because I'm dead-set against what most of them stand for. I see them as fat cats because I don't know of too many who offer their clients real value for money. Many of these accountants or lawyers are making tens of thousands of dollars a year for sometimes stitching up a deal over a three course lunch with a club chief executive—and it stinks. Ultimately they're being paid big bucks for a minimal amount of work, and the pity of it is players are bleeding to help maintain their manager's expensive lifestyle. I had a manager early on in my career because everyone kept telling me it was the right thing to do. He was pretty good, but after a few winters I realised my worth and I demanded it. The champion jockey Shane Dye follows the same principle. Dye is a person who says he likes to make the right and wrong decisions for himself ... he maintains he doesn't get dirty with himself if he chooses the wrong horse to ride, but if a manager made such a blue he'd be filthy.

Perhaps I could have squeezed an extra few thousand dollars out of the club if a manager accompanied me, but I'm being perfectly honest when I say I preferred the idea of that money being paid to a younger player than my handing it over to a manager who spends a few days out of a whole year shopping around for a deal. Ever since I turned twenty-three I've been of the belief if a club really wants you it will pay whatever you demand.

I think the only time I *really* paid for not having a manager was at the height of the ARL–Super League war when I was paid $75 000 'loyalty' money by Phillip Street while reserve graders from Manly and Wests pocketed in excess of $100 000. It wasn't the end of the world, but it was one of those lessons you never want to experience ...

Considering my stance it should come as no surprise that I for one am an advocate for major reforms in the management industry. I think Super League has taken a step in the right direction by talking about an accreditation system for managers to ensure no 'shonks' get through what has so far been a wide-open net. Both News Ltd and Phillip Street must go the extra yard, however, and introduce a scaled fee, then the most a manager could earn from a player's contract money is 5 per cent—and of the nett amount not the gross. Despite my negative feelings on managers, I believe in freedom of choice, and it is up to the individual player to decide whether he needs representation or not. If he needs a third party then my tip is he puts the bloke to work and demands the agent not only look after his football contracts but also his mortgage, tax, superannuation and any other financial matters.

Apart from that rather ordinary snake joke, whenever I think about managers I recall an old story about a boxing trainer who told his fighter before a big bout, '*We're* going to smash this bum! *We're* going to win the title! *We're* going to make millions!' He spat out all the traditional fight hype. Anyway, the kid was matched against a much better opponent and he spent the first four rounds being smashed. In between each round the trainer kept saying, '*We* can win this, come on, *we* can kill the bum!' He said that until the dazed pug looked at him and said, 'It's funny, but whenever *I* get hit *I'm* the one bleeding . . . '

Referees

Blocker Roach maintains referees are a clandestine group of men who are dirty on the world because no-one turned up to their twenty-first birthday. He reckons they vent their vindictiveness out on the footy field to ruin the party for everybody else.

It's an interesting theory, but Blocker was also the man who made the terrible blue of patting one, Eddie Ward, on the head in 1990. As a result of his actions the whole world came tumbling down around Blocker's ears, and some would say deservedly so. You see, Blocker made the terrible blunder of forgetting for one split second that out on the paddock, the referee is always boss.

Although I haven't always agreed with their decisions I've always respected the man with the whistle. Sure, there are some referees I'd love to throttle for what can only be described as lousy decisions . . . sometimes I dream of it. However, there's no point in getting into a verbal donnybrook with them because you only stand to lose. Perhaps the worse refereeing mistake I've ever witnessed occurred in the 1989 grand final, and with only two lousy minutes left on the clock. It was a heartbreaker because referee Bill Harrigan pinged Balmain's Bruce McGuire for shepherding an opposition player, but how Bruce could be penalised when Canberra's Steve Walters was running back onside is still a mystery to me. It was a decision that changed the course of the entire match. Shit, it was the difference between winning and losing a grand final . . .

Despite it often being on the tip of my tongue to jokingly ask Harrigan how his Raiders-funded condo in Queanbeyan is going these days, I rate him alongside Greg McCallum as the best referee I've played under. When Bill, a former Tactical Response Group officer, first lobbed on the refereeing scene he seemed to want to prove he was much tougher than any of the players. He came across to many of us as an arrogant so-and-so, but he's blossomed into a tremendous pro. If anything, he just wants to look prettier than the players nowdays. Queensland's Dave Manson is another referee with a thick skin but what I really admire about him is that he doesn't mind letting a game flow, and he's developed that style from having years of experience under his belt. Manson likes to give the players warnings during the run of play, such as, 'Get back on side, Balmain!' before blowing his whistle to award a penalty, and I'd be surprised if any player didn't appreciate that.

The worst possible scenario is having a referee with whom you can't communicate. Lord knows we were tested on that front during the 1990 Kangaroo tour when a French referee Monsieur Alain Sablayrolles—or 'Salad Rolls'—was given control of the Ashes series. It was a disgrace. I concluded Salad Rolls had a better command of Cantonese than of English, and trying to interpret his concept of the rules was as difficult as looking for the theme of a Swedish movie about fish. He whistled up a storm by caning us in the penalties, 17–7, the afternoon Great Britain beat us 19–12 at Wembley. I still don't know what half the penalties were for but I can say with every blast of his whistle Sablayrolles allowed the Poms to get a roll on . . . The English fans applauded the ref that dreadful day, but it's sobering to note that for the main, referees in the Old Dart are treated as public enemy No. 1—almost makes the Poms sound normal, eh? Billy Thompson, the English referee who controlled the first-ever Origin match in 1980, makes a squillion doing the rounds as a public speaker these days and he brings the house down when he tells the reason why he'd never park in the spot reserved for him on match day. 'They wondered why the spot was always vacant,' he says in his thick northern English accent. 'Well, lad, there, painted in big black letters on a white background was the bleeding word REFEREE . . . I'd have needed to buy a new car every weekend.'

On that subject, if I were a referee, my wife or kids would never be allowed to the football because I've heard the kind of things they have shouted at them from the outer. It really is cringe material. The poor bastard can't ever win. If I were one I'd take it as a great compliment to read a match report and not see my name mentioned. After all just like kids, referees should be seen but not heard.

Groupies

I've never had a problem with screaming girls throwing themselves at me or trying to rip the shirt off my back. No, I'm more popular with the older stable, the grandmothers and the mothers who want to give me a boiled fruit cake or the knitting instructions for the latest in cardigans to take home for Lee-Anne. I have heard people talk about the groupies and so-called good-time girls who hang around outside dressing rooms and then back at the Leagues Club, but I've never seen anything that would excite too many players. I refuse to believe the Rugby League scene is anything quite like it would be for professional sport in America or even the local rock 'n' roll scene. Most of the girls who follow football are mere kids who might have an innocent crush on a bloke they nominate as their pin-up boy. In such a scenario the smart blokes give them a 50 cent piece and ask the girls to phone them when they grow up.

The Media

Early in my career I used to take it very personally when there'd be a story criticising my form. I'd get furious because I had no idea of who the hell most of the blokes were in the press box and I had no idea of their credentials. I thought some of their comments were pretty harsh, especially when the former St George and Wests coach Roy Masters jumped on my case and questioned my commitment to club football. That really hurt because I was giving my all. Masters didn't know what was going on out on the field and he wasn't at our training sessions, yet he was pushing a line of thought that plenty of people wanted to embrace. As a former coach he should have known better.

As I matured I used those kinds of stories to inspire me. I'd cut out the offending article and stick it somewhere prominent, such as on the fridge, to remind myself I had a point to prove. For the main, it never ceases to amaze me how much power the press wields in Rugby League. I'm certain the tone of a story can help influence everything from representative selectors to the judiciary. It's amazing. I advise any young kid to get on the right side of the scribes quicksmart, and you do that by being respectful and understanding they have a job to do. I also believe it is best to be honest with the fourth estate because no-one likes being lied to—especially when facts are essential for their job. If you can't be fair dinkum say nothing, because most Rugby League writers are quite decent. My only criticism of them is a few haven't played Rugby League so they overlook a lot of the things that contribute to a game being a good— or a bad—match.

Mind Games

When I was at high school we studied the works of a Jesuit priest named Gerard Manley Hopkins. He penned his thoughts in the mid-to-late 1880s and while his work is considered some of the finest examples of English literature, it was all Greek to me. All except for one line he wrote on the human mind: 'O the mind has mountains; cliffs of fall, Frightful, sheer, no-man-fathomed.' It's a brilliant insight into the mind and all its complexities. There is currently a generation of sports psychologists doing their best to unravel a few mysteries of the mind. Indeed, sports psychology has emerged as one of the boom sporting industries. It seems a 'shrink' is almost considered a necessity for some of the world's top athletes. We have a bloke at Balmain named Paul Smith, and he has opened our eyes to so many good things, one of which is goal-setting. Actually, I think it's a bloody great shame they weren't in vogue when I cracked a first grade berth back in 1986, because a sports psychologist may have helped me find my feet, and voice, much quicker.

When I look back on my first four years in first grade I remember feeling inadequate. I was very light on in confidence and found it near impossible to call for the ball or override the likes of Junior, Blocker, Benny, Kerry Hemsley or Mick Neil. Despite their urgings for me to get more involved it just wasn't in my make-up to assume control of things. With time and experience, however, I became comfortable with it. I think my great turning point in that regard came in 1990 when everything fell in place and I felt confident within myself to call for shots. I sometimes wonder how much quicker I could have reached that stage if I'd had access to a sports psychologist. Once I accepted my status in the side my life became so much easier in other ways as well. For instance, when I'd drive to the ground on match day I'd get very worked up and abuse other drivers at the slightest aggravation. I dismissed it back then as pent-up aggression, but I now realise my attitude was the result of not handling the stress properly.

These days I do a lot of visualising before a game because I have found it is good to go through a game in my mind before it's played. I visualise my breaking the defensive line and setting up a team-mate with a pass; I picture myself packing down against an opponent, making my tackles and calling the shots. When I think of the power of visualising I'm often reminded of the great American golfer Ben Hogan who was almost killed on a wet Texan highway in 1949. Hogan is remembered as one of golf's meanest competitors but when he was rushed to hospital it seemed as though he wasn't going to pull through. He'd suffered some terrible injuries: a fractured pelvis, crushed ribs, a wrecked collarbone, a smashed ankle and had only a faint heartbeat. Blood clots developed in his legs and after a two-hour operation surgeons feared he'd never walk again. Well, walk he did. Almost a year to the day of his accident, Hogan climbed up the stairs to the presentation stage to receive the 1950 US Open trophy. When stunned golf reporters asked how on earth he could win the trophy after playing very little golf, Hogan told them he'd played a round *every* day he was in hospital—he simply visualised himself playing his shot.

Then there's the story of former world-rated boxer Craig Bodzinowski, who lost the lower part of his leg after a terrible motorcycle crash. From his hospital bed the pug told reporters, 'The body will receive what the mind can conceive.' Months later Bodzinowski returned to the ring and was rated No. 7 by the World Boxing Organisation, artificial leg and all. When Canberra lock Brad Clyde wrote about mental preparation in his book *Laurie and Clyde: Young Guns of Rugby League*, he quoted Dr Christiaan Barnard's belief that there is no activity in the world to which mental preparation can't be applied—and he's dead right.

Drugs

I'm anti-drugs. It doesn't matter whether they are performance-enhancing drugs or recreational drugs—I don't like them. They're not good for you. If a person allows their drug-taking to get out of control, they can take a terrible grip on their life. I found it disturbing to learn in 1993 that a NSW Drug and Alcohol Directorate survey revealed almost half of the sixteen-year-old schoolboys in the state had tried cannabis. It's a frightening thought, because it means it's so easy to get hold of drugs. As a kid I had friends who smoked marijuana, and they were good mates, but once they started smoking that stuff I lost touch with them. And my tip for any young kid who finds their friends have decided to embrace the drug culture is to drop them like a hot potato, because unless you're strong they'll drag you down into the gutter with them. Just remember you are what you consume—and dope is for dopes!

The players who cave in and take performance-enhancing drugs gain an unfair advantage over those guys who do all the right things, such as train hard and follow a sensible diet. Anyone who's been in Rugby League long enough has come across opponents who've returned from the off-season bulked up like candidates for the Mr Universe title. They're huge. Yet when asked the secret to their new look they swear it came from slurping on banana smoothies or eating banana sandwiches. It's a joke. Anyone who decides to dabble in the seedy world of steroids should be warned they're taking their life into their own hands. I've been told terrible things about what steroids have done in the past to Russian weightlifters—like cause their testicles to explode and left them as well hung as a sugar ant. If that isn't reason enough to avoid steroids at all costs, well, I don't know what is.

Alcohol

Most of the headaches I suffered when I first made grade twelve years ago came from hangovers after a big night on the town, not from jolting tackles. It amazes me how much the Rugby League culture has changed during that time. When I first lobbed at Leichhardt I can remember how some players would brag about playing and training after a big night on the soup—nowadays the players talk about the value of soya bean milk and prune juice. In the old days any first grade dressing room would be littered with buckets of icy cold beer after a game—now we're offered bottled water, platters of sandwiches and pieces of fruit to help replenish our energy levels. We're better educated these days. For instance, injured players are warned not to consume any alcohol after the first twenty-four hours of sustaining an injury because the chemicals in alcohol hinder the healing process. Yet despite all the inroads sports science has made I still don't mind the occasional night on the jibber-juice. I believe it helps build team spirit. I'll even go so far as to suggest one major reason for New South Wales' revival in the State of Origin arena can be attributed to Gus Gould's insistence we drink on a few nights of the camp away.

When Brad Fittler claimed the main attraction of Origin week for him was 'getting pissed with the boys' there was hell to pay. I understood what he meant, as would anyone who has been there. I'm afraid Freddie didn't explain himself very well and he was severely criticised by the heirarchy and some sections of the media. However, I do caution any young blokes against making the mistake of trying to be the team's centre of attention by getting smashed when he makes the big time. It can be downright embarrassing, especially for the kid.

I remember the first time my Balmain team-mate Tim Brasher made the NSW team—he got hammered. He ripped into the vodka and orange juice and let his hair down a bit too far for some people's liking. I stuck up for him and explained to everyone Timmy wasn't used to the strong stuff and thankfully they were happy to·put it down as one of those things. Actually, I've played nursemaid to a couple of the young blokes at Balmain when they've guzzled half-a-dozen drinks too many. Last season one of our boys from the bush made a real mess of himself. I thought I'd do the right thing and get him home safely. The kid looked very green around the gills so I helped him climb the stairs to his apartment and opened his door. Well, it was a typical bachelor's pad: newspapers everywhere, washing-up stuck in the sink and a pile of dirty clothes in the corner of his lounge room. And there was a cat. When the cat welcomed him home by rubbing up against his leg, the young bushie vomited all over her. It was a dreadful mess. When the kid looked at his chunder-covered feline he moaned, 'Struth Sirro, I can't remember eating *that*.'

Smoking

I tried smoking when I was a kid but I realised cigarettes couldn't be any good for me. I was lucky to kick the habit before the addiction took hold of me. These days I'm staunchly anti-smoking because I despise the fact they can cause lung, throat and tongue cancer on top of so many other illnesses. I find it of great concern that government statistics show that in 1993, 22 507 deaths were caused through smoking cigarettes—that represented 82 per cent of all drug-related deaths.

I also loathe the smell—cigarettes stink. If someone lights up in mine and Lee-Anne's vicinity when we're out enjoying a meal I see red! Surprisingly enough, there are quite a few footballers who hit the lungbusters—and they hit 'em hard. I'm told they pursue their habit at the risk of losing 5 per cent of their fitness, and the way Rugby League is heading that small percentage could be more than enough for a rival to gain an all-important edge over them. Our coach at Balmain, Wayne Pearce, has campaigned long and hard for players to kick the habit and others are following his lead. At Parramatta Brian Smith spent part of the 1996–97 off-season trying to persuade some of his 'smoking' Eels to stub out the ciggies once and for all. Smith even went to the extent of introducing a program to help wean such players as Jason Smith off the cigarettes. Brian said it didn't make sense for his players to work hard on the training paddock and then fill their lungs with smoke. I couldn't agree more.

Injuries

Rugby League is a rugged game and we'd be living in a fantasy world to think a person could be pile-driven into the ground, smacked about the head or have their body twisted at unnatural angles and escape without any injury. I had a pretty good run in my first five years of grade but when reality bit in 1991, it sunk its teeth in nice and deep. I needed a knee reconstruction in the winter of '91 after I fell awkwardly in a tackle and damaged my posterior cruciate. Even though the recovery was quite brutal I guess we modern-day players are much luckier than previous generations because such an injury would have spelled the end of a player's career twenty years ago. I've had other battles to fight, such as a bulging disc in my lower back, a groin injury, a broken thumb, and I've needed my elbow and knee scraped.

One of the worst things a footballer must do is play with injuries. I don't think too many guys ever play a whole season 100 per cent fit. It's a definite risk, but normally there isn't much choice. Even if most players had the choice of playing or not playing despite an injury, I reckon they would. I did when I had a groin injury in 1987 and I didn't enjoy it at all—it was a bastard of a time. I would've loved to have been able to rest, but I didn't dare ask Billy Anderson for a break because I didn't want to seem like a big head. Nevertheless, it was bloody painful and my form suffered and people started to question my worth to the Tigers.

In saying that, however, I'm adamant once a player is injured he owes it to his team to do everything he possibly can to get back on the paddock. But even that must be plotted carefully—I bought a backswing a few years ago in the mistaken belief it would help relieve the pressure from my bulging disc. A professional footballer must talk to his doctor, understand how the injury occurred, how it is best treated and what can be done to avoid it happening again. The offshoot to an injury that has sidelined a player for a few weeks is he favours the problem area, and that is only natural. However, to steal a line from Laurie Daley it is sometimes better to get back on the wild horse that bucked you off. The Canberra ace reckons a player fresh from the comeback trail will be hammered if he goes about his business half-heartedly, and I reckon he's spot on.

Diet

You are what you eat, and I have to say I know a few blokes who eat plenty of rump! I don't mind the occasional binge on junk food, but I don't think there is any way a player can gorge himself on all the wrong foods and expect to play like a superstar. I load up on carbohydrates close to match day and watch what I eat in the earlier part of the week. Once again, I've been spoiled rotten by having someone like Wayne Pearce at the club because he can tell me such things as Atlantic salmon is good for my heart or that baked beans are rich in fibre. That kind of information is so important, because while you can do all the training in the world, it will fall in a heap if the main source of your diet comes from a takeaway food outlet.

My normal day of eating is:

Breakfast

4 crushed Weetbix mixed with banana or strawberry and lite white milk
2 pieces of toast with jam or vegemite (no butter)
1 cup of tea with lite white milk

Lunch

2 chicken and salad rolls (brown bread, no butter)
1 small fruit salad
1 piece of low fat carrot cake

Dinner
Chicken and rice dish
or
Barbecued lean cuts of meat

I normally drink eight big glasses of water throughout the course of a day or enjoy a diet soda if I feel like a bit of a change. I can't stress the benefit from eating at least three pieces of fresh fruit a day.

I find it quite strange that obesity is becoming a major problem in Australia because we have a fabulous climate for outdoor activities, our fruit ranks among the world's best for quality and nutritious foods are readily available from almost everywhere. Yet, it seems as though we've become a nation of couch potatoes who can't get enough of saturated fat into our system while watching television. It is a great pity. What really concerns me is going to schools and being confronted with roly-poly kids who are obviously not only eating all the wrong tucker but are doing hardly any exercise. It's a problem that must be addressed or our health system will be inundated with obesity-related illnesses such as high blood pressure, diabetes, heart disease and even by people complaining of sore knees from supporting too many unnecessary kilos of blubber.

THE SUPER LEAGUE STRUGGLE

CHAPTER 19

I've been bailed up by what seems to have been hundreds of people over the past two years who have wanted to know whether their game will ever be the same again. They're worried by the terrible hammering Rugby League has taken during the long and bitter Super League war and I'm afraid my answer to them is, 'I don't know'. As you'd imagine, however, I'm desperately hoping things will return to the way they were before 1 April 1995, the day Super League's John Ribot declared war on Phillip Street. Unfortunately it was no April Fool's Day joke. By sunset that evening a red line had been drawn straight down the middle of Rugby League and two groups—the loyalists and the rebels—had been formed. Two years on and it's my great hope an armistice can soon be brokered because I'm of the opinion that a compromise is the only way we're going to stop the game from bleeding. At the time of writing I believe both competitions have managed to hang in because the playing standard on both sides of the fence has been pretty good.

In the ARL's Optus Cup most people judged our games to be extremely competitive because the likes of Balmain, Souths and the South Queensland Crushers had applied plenty of acid to the high-profile teams such as Manly, Easts and Parramatta. From the feedback I've received I believe the punters are more than happy with our efforts. As for Super League, well, I refute Phil Gould's allegations that those games were played without passion. Knowing some of the guys who play in that organisation, such as Glenn Lazarus, Brad Clyde, Laurie Daley, Mark Geyer and Andrew Ettingshausen, there's no way they'd turn it up or play in a Mickey Mouse competition. And as a bloke who's coached them for the NSW Origin side, Phil should've known much better. Unfortunately, every time somebody takes a pot shot such as Gus's 'no passion' cry, it makes it that little bit harder for the two parties to get back together. For the record I watched a few Super League games on television and some of them were crackers, such as their opening round match between Canberra and Cronulla. It was played at breakneck pace and I enjoyed it a lot . . . you'd have to be a hard marker not to appreciate their skill and athleticism.

Nevertheless, I consider the split to be one hell of a tragedy, and I deeply regret that Phillip Street and a delegation from News Ltd haven't managed to get together and smoke the peace pipe. There were encouraging rumours that Optus and Foxtel had plans to get together and sort out a deal that would unify the game, but there has been nothing concrete to hang a hat on. While passions were running high, one thing I couldn't understand throughout the war was the amount of personal sniping that went on. We witnessed some old friendships, such as the thirty-something year bond between former ARL boss Ken Arthurson and ex-Canterbury supremo Peter Moore crumble, and why? Friendships should never have come into play. If anyone had expected me to bag my mates Andrew Ettingshausen or Laurie Daley for joining Super League they'd have been very disappointed. I'm certain they believed they were doing the right thing throwing their weight behind the News Ltd competition.

If we were to pinpoint the one thing that *really* damaged the game, it was the lengthy court cases which not only dragged on but occupied plenty of media space. People grew tired of the never-ending drama and they switched off from the footy and tuned into other sports such as basketball and Aussie Rules. And it isn't hard to realise why the average fan took exception to the amounts of money being thrown about by both groups to recruit talent. Most of the game's diehard supporters were battling to survive on four-or-five hundred bucks a week, and I can see how it would have seemed obscene to them because they have to work hard for forty-hours a week while we footballers were being paid thousands for our 'loyalty'.

I first heard whispered rumours about Super League forming on the 1994 Kangaroo tour. I initially dismissed the talk as a pipedream because I couldn't see how anyone would be able to afford to shell out millions of bucks to assume control of the game. How wrong was I? The rumours of a rebel competition backed by one of the world's richest men, Rupert Murdoch, gained great momentum when ARL chairman Ken Arthurson flew home from the Kangaroo tour to try to squash any threat before he had a World Series Cricket-type situation on his hands. My concern about Balmain's position in a game that seemed destined to plunge into turmoil escalated when a journalist interviewed my roomie Glenn Lazarus to get his views on what a rebel competition would mean to him and his Brisbane team-mates.

Lazzo must have forgotten I was in the room when he told the scribe it would be great for him not to have to play 'nothing' games against the likes of Balmain, the Gold Coast and Souths. I wasn't overly offended by his dismissing Balmain as a force in '94 because we did have an ordinary season . . . although I will stress we were operating on a skinny $2 million budget compared to the Broncos' fat $6 million. But, crickey, we were a foundation club . . . the Tigers were there in 1908 . . . and I found it quite disturbing that going by Lazzo's reaction it seemed as though we could be disregarded by some people with a mere wave of their hand. While I wrestled with where Balmain stood in the war, other guys, such as Canberra's David Furner, had their own demons to contend with. As a member of a Super League-aligned club Dave had a bloody tough decision to make because his old man, Don, was a high-profile official with the ARL. I didn't envy him his position but in the end he decided to do what most players opted for—to remain with their team-mates. At least it didn't tear the Furner household apart because Don, a former national coach and ARL selector, told the press he was happy to live with his son's decision.

As for the Super League concept itself, I thought there were some credible ideas, such as the World Club Challenge; the promise of paying injured players the full amount of their contract; providing comprehensive health insurance plans for all players and their dependants; and instigating a superannuation fund to help prepare the players for a secure financial future. Super League also based a team in Adelaide and that has proven to be a success story. They sold plenty of season passes and their inaugural crowd of 27 000 suggested they'd pulled the right rein by opening up new Rugby League territory. I viewed a lot of the Super League initiatives as positive stuff and they had plenty of merit. Like many people, however, I didn't appreciate the cloak and dagger way in which the Super League officials went about recruiting players.

Kiwi centre Jarrod McCracken was one guy who signed a deal with the News Ltd backed organisation because he claimed John Ribot gave him an ultimatum to sign, now or never. McCracken was to later claim under oath in another courtroom battle that he signed the contract under severe duress. After many months of deliberation the judge decided to overturn McCracken's contract and that paved the way for him to join the ARL. He suffered some grave consequences for his actions, however. He fell out of favour with his coach Chris Anderson, he was isolated by the Bulldogs hierarchy and he missed out on a grand final winner's medal because he was cut from the club just weeks before the Bulldogs pulled off an amazing victory over red-hot favourites, Manly. McCracken may have cleaned up at Phillip Street with a deal that set him up for life, but he certainly lost out in many other ways . . .

Embattled ARL chief executive Ken Arthurson likened the News Ltd raid on Phillip Street to the Japanese bombing raid on Pearl Harbor in 1942. He rallied his loyal forces to fight a rearguard action, but just like the American defenders at Hawaii over fifty years ago, the ARL failed to notice some early warning signals. They must have realised in the late '80s and early '90s that many players were disgruntled by what was perceived as the League's idea of priorities. For instance, on the 1990 Kangaroo tour we players couldn't believe it when the team management said we'd be responsible for paying for our own laundry and any extra meals. We saw that as a joke because the officials were travelling first class, they were staying in plush five star hotels, they were wining and dining in the swankiest restaurants in England and they didn't mind bending their elbows at the bar—all on the ARL account. In the twelve weeks I was in northern England and southern France I forked out over $1000 on telephone calls to Lee-Anne and family men such as Blocker spent $2000 or more on keeping in touch with their wives and kids, yet we weren't being compensated for any of that. The seeds for discontent were also planted when we players realised the League was raking in millions of dollars for the television rights for the State of Origin in the late '80s and early '90s but none of it was being filtered down to the blokes who were getting battered and bruised.

As for me, I'm of the opinion I was an afterthought when the ARL paid me $75 000 while they paid out $200 000 for guys who'd only just cracked a first grade berth. I was pretty disheartened by their idea of a 'good deal' for a Test player. But enough said on that. The funny sidelight was two days after it was reported in the newspaper that I'd signed on with Phillip Street my old Tigers team-mate Benny Elias bailed me up in the street and asked which camp I intended to align myself with. When I told the little bloke I'd just signed a deal with the ARL he hit his forehead with his hands and cursed in Arabic. Benny said he and News Ltd heavy Ken Cowley were close mates and he probably could have worked a great deal for me. Well, I didn't know whether it was Benny just trying to get me going, so I said 'Thanks, mate' and got on with my business.

And that's exactly what the ARL and Super League have to do now, get on with business. If they should ever get together it's going to take a lot of negotiating and a lot of leeway on both sides to form a compromise. I think one of the great assets Phillip Street has is John Quayle's replacement, Neil Whittaker. I have a lot of faith in the former Balmain forward doing the right thing by the game because he has a genuine love for Rugby League. One of Neil's great strengths is he doesn't have any of the emotion that made it too difficult for Quayle, Ribot, Arthurson and Cowley to see eye-to-eye.

As an ARL-loyal player I was quite miffed to see official after official leave Phillip Street once the Supreme Court decided to allow Super League to kick off in 1996. The voices we'd all heard maintain the rage throughout the war fell silent as they abandoned their posts for what was reported to be personal reasons. Naturally, I don't blame Ken Arthurson for bowing out. He fought a good fight, and by the time he decided to put his heels up you could hear in his voice that he was genuinely exhausted. Another bloke who gained my total admiration was Geoff Carr, Phillip Street's National Premiership Communications Manager. He stuck by his guns and he was genuinely concerned how we players would be affected by the outcome of the war.

Now it's time for the players and the political animals involved in the new environment to show some concern for the game itself. Unless we get together, and soon, there might not be a game for boys like my two sons Curtis and Bayley to play in the future.

THE FAMILY MAN

CHAPTER 20

There have been quite a few times when I've felt guilty about the many sacrifices my wife Lee-Anne has been forced to endure while I've pursued my football career. I've always tried to justify what I do by thinking Rugby League is helping me to set up my wife Lee-Anne and our two beautiful boys Curtis and Bayley for life. That logic is occasionally challenged however, like the time Lee-Anne had her tonsils taken out while I was overseas representing Australia and the night I telephoned her when I was on the 1990 Kangaroo tour. It was around midnight in Sydney and I could tell by her voice that she was terrified because she'd spied a HUUUUUUGE spider lurking in our bedroom. Normally I'd have made a joke of it and said something smart like 'Quick love, ring the cops!', but being on the other side of the world and not being able to do anything made me feel so bloody *helpless*. All I could do was ring someone and ask them to go around to our house and kill the spider. Take it from me, having your wife crying on the other end of the blower is the worst thing possible for a Kangaroo stuck in England's industrial north.

Throughout this book I've raved on about the importance of gaining the green and gold jumper, the disappointment of playing in *two* losing grand final sides, the pride in wearing the black and gold and the thrill of winning a few awards for playing football. When I look around, however, it doesn't take much time for me to realise my most valued trophies in life are Lee-Anne, Bayley and Curtis—*they're* the ones who have made all the bumps, the breaks and the occasional disappointments worth the effort. We have a happy little family. Lee-Anne is everything you'd expect from a loving mother, a wife and best friend, three-year-old Curtis is a little legend, and Bayley has a healthy set of lungs—if he doesn't get a job as a car alarm when he gets older he'll be a bloody good opera singer.

I don't intend to push either of the boys into football, but I'll definitely support whatever interest they decide to pursue, be it golf, tennis, soccer or whatever. As long as the boys are healthy and happy, I'll be a pretty contented bloke. I think Curtis is going to be quite a big boy when he grows up, but we'll have to get stuck into some extra tackling practice soon because the poor little critter was tackled by Danny Stains's boy, Izaak, at the Balmain Leagues Club recently and as soon as he hit the ground he started bawling—and yeah, I know some critics will say he inherited that trait from his old man!

As for critics, I've not known a tougher one in my time than Lee-Anne. She has been with me ever since I was given my call-up to first grade in 1986 and, boy, if she ever thinks I haven't put in during a game she really rips and tears with a ferocity that I never saw in the likes of Warren Ryan or Bobby Fulton. And it is based on my getting the rounds of the kitchen table that I say God help the boys if any of their future school reports should mention they aren't putting in enough effort in the classroom!

LEE-ANNE'S SAY

CHAPTER 21

I tell everyone I have three kids: Curtis, Bayley and then the biggest handful of them all, Sirro. We went to the same school but we didn't ever speak to one another until at a chance meeting in a nightclub a few years after we graduated. I can remember thinking how shy Paul was despite his size and his also being a police officer. He had worked on the Council with my uncle so it took only a phone call for me to find out what kind of a person Mr Sironen really was—and he passed the test with flying colours.

Paul isn't a naturally aggressive person, he has to build himself up to be angry. When we first started going out it concerned me that on the morning of a match he used to try and start an argument, and it left me feeling very angry and confused. Once I realised what he was doing—building himself up for the game—I decided to let him have it with both barrels, and the first time I retaliated I think Paul didn't know what to do. He's mellowed in his older age. These days he has our baby boys Curtis and Bayley demanding his attention on the morning of the game, and much to our neighbours' delight our household has really quietened down on match day.

As for being a good father, Paul does his best. His football and work commitments take huge chunks out of his day and when he spends time with the kids he's always out to give them as much as he possibly can and I dread it when I hear him whisper, 'Hey Curtis, do you wanna rumble?' The kids are number one with him, however, and I'm sure as they grow Paul will be as much a mate to them as a dad.

As a husband? Well, Sirro isn't the type to bowl me over with too many surprises, such as a bunch of flowers. Even the night he proposed to me was no surprise because, true to form, he jabbered his way through it. Rather than simply asking me to marry him he went through every reason why he couldn't propose to me in the way he would have preferred. For instance, he couldn't put a note in my meal as he would have liked because he feared I'd have choked on it. He didn't want to buy me a ring because he didn't know whether I'd like it . . . And there were other reasons but we were married anyway.

Paul and I are very good friends and very much in love. I'm glad I was with him just before he started playing first grade because it's been special to share the highlights of his career, and the occasional low point. Being a football widow isn't always fun, there are many lonely moments. But I've tried to be understanding because I know that apart from enjoying himself Paul considers his playing the best way to set up the family for life.

Going to the football has been interesting because I've always had to bite my tongue when someone yells out something bad about the big fellow. As much as I would love to put them back in their place, I wouldn't dare embarrass Paul by arguing with them. Curtis also doesn't understand why some things happen at the game—he's forever asking me, 'Why did that man tackle Daddy?' or 'Why are the people booing him?' It's all very innocent.

Paul has all that to look forward to when he hangs up his boots because I'll be getting back into netball and touch football. By then, I'm sure the boys will be able to look after him because, as I've already said, he's a much bigger kid than either of them.

PROFILE

CHAPTER 22

Full name: Paul Ilmari Sironen.

Birthdate: 23 May 1965.

Birthplace: North Sydney.

First football team: Gladesville Bowling and Sports Club.

First position: I can't believe the coach did this to me, but he threw me up front as a prop. If ever there was a brutal initiation then this was it because I was only six and had no idea of what I was doing.

Other sports: Cricket and athletics. I reckon my dad would have loved for me to represent Australia at the Olympics in either the shot-put or javelin.

Schools: East Ryde Primary, Malvina High and Holy Cross at Ryde.

First job: Cook at McDonald's. I'll let you in on a little secret here, the special sauce was really my sweat!

Current job: Sales and marketing for SportM Sportswear. My boss is the former referee Chris Ward, and I reckon our working together proves a fox and a hound can get along.

Favourite coach: Warren 'Wok' Ryan because he brought the best out in me.

Hardest tackler: I find it hard to go past Manly's David Gillespie. Even though he's getting long in the tooth the big fella still knows where to find the sweet spot.

Favourite ground: Leichhardt Oval. The atmosphere and the people have always meant a lot to me.

Least favourite ground: Without doubt, Penrith Park. I don't think I've ever won a game there. My initiation to the place was also pretty tough—a member of their Jersey Flegg team gave me an evil Christmas hold.

Team I least like playing: Newcastle. They have stinging defence and then they run the ball like Kamikaze pilots into the line.

Best referee: Bill Harrigan. He's fit, he can talk to the players, and best of all he has the courage of his convictions.

My greatest honour: Playing for Australia.

Grand final record: Two appearances. No laps of honour.

Kangaroo tours: Three—1986, 1990 and 1994.

Worst injury: A knee reconstruction—the recovery was bloody brutal.

My hardest rival: Newcastle's Paul Harragon always puts up a good fight.

Which celebrity would I most like to be stuck on a tropical island with?: Movie star Kim Bassinger, on the proviso she could catch fish and crack coconuts.

Which Rugby League identity would make the best prime minister?: Big Mal Meninga. He's already at Canberra so it would at least save the taxpayers the removalist's bill.

As an Australian which issue most concerns me?: The seemingly ever-increasing crime rate ... it's getting too far out of hand.

If I wasn't a footballer what would I be doing?: I'd probably be a 25 stone sergeant behind a desk in some country station.

My childhood heroes: Test cricketer Dennis Lillee for his fighting spirit and Manly fullback Graham Eadie.

Am I superstitious?: I'm more forgetful than superstitious and that's why I check my kitbag twice before I leave home on match day.

Ideal meal: A huge seafood platter at the Pan Roma restaurant in Leichhardt.

Meal from hell: It would have to be anything Wayne Pearce would dish up ... lentils, mung beans and the like.

Favourite musicians: Elton John, SuperTramp and Dragon.

Noise pollution: Getting stuck in a lift with Terry Hill.

Ideal holiday: Hawaii. It offers so much from sandy beaches to glamorous nightclubs.

How would I like to be remembered as a footballer?: As a bloke who tried hard and enjoyed himself.

Paul Sironen

CLUB CAREER (Record does not include 1997 season)

	Games	Tries	Points
Balmain Tigers			
1985–96	204	21	84

REPRESENTATIVE CAREER

CITY-COUNTRY

	Games	Tries	Points
City Seconds 1986	1	-	0
City Origin 1987–94	7	-	0
TOTAL	8	-	0

NEW SOUTH WALES

	Games	Tries	Points
State of Origin 1989–96	14	-	0

AUSTRALIA

	Games	Tries	Points
Tests 1986–94	21	3	12
World Cup 1988–92	2	-	0
Tour Matches 1986–94	26	2	8
TOTAL	49	5	20

GRAND TOTAL

	Games	Tries	Points
All Senior matches	275	26	104

INDIVIDUAL HONOURS

- Dally M Rookie of the Year 1986
- NSW Rugby League Writers' Discovery of the Year 1986
- Dally M Second Rower of the Year
- He is only one of four forwards to tour three times with the Kangaroos (1986, 1990, 1994). The others were Wally Prigg, Noel Kelly and Johnny Raper.

THE SIRRO ROAST

CHAPTER 23

P aul Sironen has made a tremendous impression on some of the modern game's greatest players. He has represented Australia, New South Wales and Balmain with great distinction—and with a huge smile on his face. Below, some of Paul's contemporaries take time out to say what they think gave Sirro an edge as a player and a bloke.

Wayne Pearce, Balmain captain and coach: To talk about Paul Sironen is to talk about one of the most popular players in the game. Not only is he a good friend but he's also a great player. Strong team spirit means a lot to him and from a team-mate's perspective he's very important because he knows how to make the players laugh. As for his contribution as a player, since I took over as the Tigers coach in 1994 Sirro has been a tower of strength and he's developed into a tremendous leader.

Steve Roach, Balmain: I'm mad about the bloke. I've never known any player who loves touring life like big Sirro because he's always got a big grin on his dial. As for his dedication to playing footy, well, the greatest thing I can say about Paul is he has given his all for the Tigers when he was the only 'name' forward. It's easy to play well when you have a bit of support but Sirro was a definite one-man band for a few years.

Tim Brasher, Balmain 1988–97: Paul has earned respect over the years because of the way he plays his football, but plenty of players think of him warmly because he is a good-hearted bloke ... and he's a funny bloke. When I first made the NSW side I was very nervous and I didn't know what to expect but the sight of him on the microphone helped put my fears to rest. I'll never forget the afternoon in the mid-1990s when Balmain was going through a lean stretch and we were getting hammered by Canberra down at their home ground. Through some inspired football we clawed our way back and as I kicked a goal from the sideline to draw the game, I heard from some of the other guys that Sirro had jumped up and down like a little kid when he saw the ball go straight through the posts. I asked him about it later in the dressing room and he gave an impromptu show of jumping up and down; however, because the dressing room floor had tiles he slipped, fell on his butt and then cracked his head on the floor!

Glenn Morrison, Balmain 1996–97: When I first came down to Sydney from the Central Coast I was amazed by Paul Sironen because he's just as much a comedian as he is a great footballer. However, Sirro is one bloke who knows when to cut out his clowning about and switch on. As a young player one of the best lessons I've learned from Sirro is there is room for some fun in professional Rugby League. As for his onfield efforts, I am amazed by the bloke because he's always about to take that extra hit-up when he's needed.

Ellery Hanley, Balmain 1988 and 96–97: I am pleased to say I have played alongside Paul Sironen because he is a gentleman and I have a huge amount of respect for him. He has played tremendously for Balmain and he has represented his country well. I can't speak highly enough about him as a player because in the half-dozen internationals I've played against him, he certainly hit me very hard with some great tackles.

Bill Anderson, Balmain coach 1987: I coached Paul after he returned from the 1986 Kangaroo tour and he had a few problems. He was carrying a bit of weight, he had a groin injury and I think he was also a bit star-struck after touring Great Britain and France, and even though he struggled he had a reasonable year. Some of the best football I've seen Paul play was in 1996, however, when he led from the front row . . . it was very inspiring. I believe he once went with the flow when it came to talking about football, but he is now at a stage where he can talk about any issue with a great authority. Sirro is a tremendous clubman and everyone welcomes his great sense of humour.

Brad Clyde, NSW and Australian team-mate: The first time I roomed with Sirro for New South Wales I walked into the room and wanted to walk straight out again because he was singing along to Neil Diamond's 'Solitary Man' and he was belting it out at the top of his voice. He didn't bat an eyelid when I walked in and then as the song finished he went straight into 'Sweet Caroline'. I didn't know what to do, and I didn't want to encourage him by clapping or anything silly.

Andrew Ettingshausen, NSW and Australian team-mate: There are a million-and-one Paul Sironen stories circulating out there and so it's a struggle to pinpoint that *one* funny one that stands out from all the rest. Sirro's standing in the game is such that most players think of him with a tremendous amount of respect. And that isn't derived from his simply being a funny bloke or a guy who plays football well—it comes from his being seen as a good man with a good heart.